A Tent in the Wilderness

A Journey of Joy, Misery and Adventure

By Jack Chambless

Cover image © Shutterstock.com

www.innovativeinkpublishing.com
Send all inquiries to:
4050 Westmark Drive
Dubuque, IA 52004-1840

Published in the United States of America

For Gabriel—Thank you for being an incredible son who inspires us every day to enjoy everything good that life has to offer.

Contents

Introduction vii

CHAPTER 1: It Is Called Wildlife for a Reason 1

CHAPTER 2: Camping with—and Anywhere Near—Humans 13

CHAPTER 3: Rain, Lightning, and 108 MPH Winds 23

CHAPTER 4: Suffering without Silence...39

CHAPTER 5: The Best Parts of Tent Camping................................55

CHAPTER 6: A Place for Healing and Reflection............................79

THE LONELY TAVERN...87

Introduction

My first memory of temporarily living in a tent had nothing to do with fun or relaxation. In fact, it was the farthest thing from it.

Sometime in the spring of 1974 I found myself lying on my back staring down at all ten of my toes that were bleeding and crooked. I suppose it was for the best that all I could see were my feet because my head had a large gash in it that had my mother and her friend in full-on hysterics.

Only minutes earlier, I had been sitting on my bicycle on top of an exceptionally large hill near the campground of Pine Creek Lake in southeastern Oklahoma.

My father, a budding professional bass-fisherman at the time, had taken my family on a tent camping adventure while he roared off every morning on his boat to fish a tournament.

Since it was the 1970s, after he took off for his day, I got on my bike wearing cutoff blue jean shorts (a staple of youth attire at that time), no shoes, no socks, no shirt, no helmet, or protective gear of any kind. I am not even sure that other than my hero, Evel Knievel, anyone else in America wore helmets to do anything other than play football.

I am certain no kid in America wore helmets when bike riding. The 1970s meant freedom. Youngsters in the United States during that time were regarded like feral hogs who roamed the countryside, rarely observed, to do whatever we wanted.

So, it was with that natural, non-helicopter parent model, that I rode my bike with some new friends I had made to the top of a steep, long, curvy hill and peered out over the kingdom of stunt-riding I had inherited.

I watched as other kids, mostly older than me, successfully flew down this hill at what seemed like the speed of sound and navigated the long turn at the bottom.

"Come on! It's great!" I am sure I heard someone say as I readied myself.

Somewhere between the top of what felt like Oklahoma's Mt. Everest and the bottom of that hill my bike began to do something funny.

For some reason, my handlebar began to shake violently side to side and with it, my front tire. Having not yet studied the physics of traveling 80 mph downhill on a two-wheeled object from Wal-Mart, all I knew was that the law of gravity was about to take over.

Sure enough, the front tire lurched abruptly to the right, and I sailed over the handlebars and toward the asphalt below.

According to the kids who witnessed what could have been an all-time YouTube moment, the first thing on my body to contact Earth was my noggin.

I recall, to this day, rolling head over heels the rest of the way. Once this stopped at the bottom of the hill I stood up and noticed that the half dozen or so kids waiting for me were all staring with their eyes and mouths agape.

Three seconds later they scattered like quail.

All of them but one took off because, being normal youths, there is no way they wanted to be in the vicinity of someone who could point at them and say, "Mom, he is the one who told me to do it. . . . "

The one person who ran to get help was a young girl who was part of a family we went camping with. Normally, she and I did not get along well, but she was my savior that day.

By the time she found my mother, I was staggering down the road covered in blood and embarrassment.

The next thing I knew I was in our tent wondering why my toes looked like ten mangled Vienna sausages.

My mother—who could pass for an angel—took care of me in her usual kind, loving, and tender way while I was screaming my head off.

Then, one of the worst things that could happen, happened.

Big Jack walked into the tent.

My dad's day-to-day demeanor was not unlike that of a Kodiak Bear with hemorrhoids or a severely ingrown toenail.

The nanosecond he unzipped that old Coleman tent he demanded that everyone be quiet. I think the birds in the forest within a five-mile radius of that tent stopped chirping.

My dad took me to his truck, and off to the hospital we went. By that Monday I was the coolest kid in the second grade of Eugene Field Elementary School as I showed off my stitches and partially shaved head.

I was also unwittingly at the beginning of what has been more than fifty years of a tent camping life that has, at times, bordered on the absurd, but has rarely, if ever, been boring.

1

It Is Called Wildlife for a Reason

I am one of those unfortunate beings who lives within what is called a "Metropolitan area." That means there are humans, over 2.6 million of them, to be exact, all around me. It also means that most of the people I encounter would rather walk across burning coals than sleep in a tent in the wilderness.

When I engage in conversations with these city-loving, frequently bathed, and nicely dressed suburbanites, the subject of travel often comes up.

"Wait, you are going where and doing what??" is the most common question I get when I explain my wife's and my plans to leave civilization behind.

As I try to share my view of how overrated human contact is and how valuable nature is to restoring sanity and greater health, the first query I hear is, "But what about wild animals?"

Ah, yes . . . wild animals.

For some reason, my life as a tent camper seems to have coincided with memos that are sent out to the animal kingdom that our family is coming to their headquarters. Those animals that read these memos do not usually take the form of rabbits and butterflies.

Rather, it is the larger ones—sometimes the kind that can reduce or disfigure the human population—that I seem to attract.

During the summer of 2001 I was on a trip with my wife, Sarah, and our two small sons, Gehrig and Gabriel, to Shenandoah National Park in Virginia. Gehrig was two and his little brother Gabriel was a chubby nine-month-old infant.

Sarah and I had worked out an arrangement a couple of years earlier whereby we would share tent camping workloads based on the principle of comparative advantage.

As an economics professor by trade, I was able to explain to her that since I got a D-minus in geometry in high school and she earned an A in honors geometry, she should always oversee putting up the tent since she had, compared to me, an advantage in this type of activity. My brain simply does not process three-dimensional construction, opposing motions, or projects that have multiple angles involved.

But I can gather firewood and I can cook meat over the fire it produces. This sort of primitive, low I.Q. task is right up my alley.

Having been born in Germany and greatly influenced by my German mother, I also know how to clean up well, so dishwashing is also part of my comparative advantage.

One night in Shenandoah we had just finished dinner when we got into an argument about something. I do not remember the details of what the argument was about, but I seem to recall her being wrong about something, so in a huff I got up and started for the tent.

When she asked me about the dishes, I said something along the lines of, "You do them, I am going to bed," like any immature husband would do.

Well, not being German and having already done her part by putting up the tent, Sarah decided to make a half-hearted, resentful effort when putting away the remaining food and cleaning up after we ate.

Somewhere around 2 a.m. I heard a very loud, banging noise outside of our tent.

When I peered out, I saw an enormous black bear—lower half on the ground, upper half on the picnic table—helping my wife finish putting away the leftover food.

Somewhere between gently and wildly shaking her, I woke my wife up and said, in a somewhat panicked tone, "Sarah! There is a bear outside! What the hell did you do with the food??!?"

When my wife hits her personal panic button, she, according to me and my sons, always looks like a Claymation chicken character from the movie *Chicken Run* that attempts to fly but just sits there bobbing up and down flapping their wings.

Sarah does not have wings but when she loses it, she flaps anyway and attempts to fly.

As she was in flight mode she frantically said, "Well, some of it is in the fire, some is wrapped up in your sweatshirt and the dishes are on the table!"

Now I felt my wings beginning to flap. . . .

Lovingly (I think), but with great urgency, I informed her that we were sleeping in the clothes we cooked and ate in and when this bear was finished outside its next stop would be our tent where her precious children—and one stupid husband—were also residing.

This might be a good time to mention that one of my "hobbies" when we pitch a tent is to find wood that I can whittle while relaxing on what are supposed to be bear-free vacations. For this I use a Bowie knife with a nice, sharp 4.5" blade.

Realizing that I had a form of protection nearby, Sarah's next suggestion was quite logical.

"Take a weapon out there in case you have to fight the bear."

Maybe it was the Ballad of Davy Crockett (after all the song says that he "Kilt him a b'ar when he was only three") that made her think I was suited for this type of conflict or perhaps it seemed better than suggesting I use a frying pan. I do not know.

In her frantic state, her question was clearly more about saving her sons than caring about the rights of this hungry animal—even though we were the imbeciles that encouraged his visit to begin with.

.01 seconds after she put in her request, I exclaimed, "Are your crazy? If I go out in a National Park campground full of people and kill a bear, I'll go to prison!"

Without reflection, blinking, or the passing of 1/10 of a second, she blurted out,

"For how long?"

You might want to take a moment to re-read the last line because that is precisely the incredible response this lady came up with.

I must hand it to her. She was a brilliant economics major in college. A foundational principle of economics is to understand cost-benefit analysis. To her, this was simple.

<u>Benefit of husband having a knife vs. claw fight with a bear</u>: Children survive.

<u>Cost of husband winning this fight with a bear</u>: Husband goes to prison for X number of days/months/years/decades.

All she was asking me to do at that moment was provide an estimate of how many days/months/years I would be in Alcatraz, and she would therefore be able to determine if it would be rational to carry out her proposal.

Fortunately for me, a couple of seconds later the bear put his foot on the little amount of hot embers left in the firepit while trying to retrieve some baked beans. He took off quickly but left a huge mess.

I spent the rest of the night sitting on top of the picnic table in case he decided to come back. I also found my favorite University of Oklahoma sweatshirt with a big, muddy paw print on the front—sort of an autograph, I suppose.

"For how long . . . what the hell does that mean?" is the question that kept rolling through my brain while I stared at the tent that the bear did not enter.

I let her sleep peacefully until the sun first appeared over the mountains. Then, I went back into the tent, woke her up as kindly as I could, and asked her what "For how long?" means.

"Well, I thought they might put you in jail for a night," was her lame answer.

On our way out of Shenandoah we casually brought up ending the life of bears in self-defense with a park employee who not so casually indicated that the penalty would be somewhere in between life in prison without parole and lethal injection.

From that day forward I have made sure that the dishes are washed before we go to bed.

Speaking of bears, let me introduce you to my brother—a fine young man who almost got me eaten in Wyoming back in the summer of 2001 when we were on our first (and last) backcountry camping vacation as siblings.

Our trip was doomed to fail before we took one step on a trail.

When we met in Salt Lake City and drove from there to the Tetons, we did so with the understanding that I was furnishing the tent. What I did not tell him was that I did not know how to put up _my own tent._

My brother is a very skilled handyman and home-remodeling type that guys like me hate with a passion.

So, logically I deduced that he would be able to put up his brother's tent.

We arrived in the Tetons well past midnight. I pulled out the tent, handed it to him and then informed him that not only did I not know how to put up my tent, but I also had no interest in learning how to.

He was so tired—and disgusted—that instead of cooperating and doing what his brother was incapable of doing, he refused to help.

So, we stretched out on the ground, used the tent (with some poles sticking out of it) as a large sheet and passed out.

At about 7 a.m. I heard a lot of laughing nearby.

For some reason, the other campers who saw us could not help enjoying our (my) ineptitude.

My brother, interestingly enough, was not laughing. . . .

Later that day we made it to the ranger headquarters to see about getting our backcountry camping permits.

Having hiked and camped in the Tetons and Yellowstone in 1999 I was adamant that he listen carefully to the experts issuing us our permits when they began speaking about grizzly bears—and how to avoid seeing them up close.

When the ranger got to the part about making noise as you hike in the mountains of this park, I kept looking at my brother and nodding to lend a "this is really important" ambiance to this meeting.

The next day we finished loading our packs and headed out for a three-day brothers-only trip that we had, to that point, never participated in.

Somewhere around the first hour into our walking journey I shouted the favorite phrase Sarah and I use when we hike in grizzly territory.

"WHOOOOAAA BEAR!" I loudly pronounced. Then, a few seconds later, I did it again.

Visibly perturbed, my younger sibling turned around and said, "Would you please shut up?"

"Didn't you hear the ranger say we needed to make noise?" I asked.

"I have never seen a grizzly bear and I would like to see one," was his reply.

So, to help him have a rare, good time away from home, for the rest of the three-day trip my "Whoa Bear" commentary was severely limited though I did manage to mumble, "You have got to be kidding me . . . " many times for the next three days.

And then it happened. . . .

On day three we were coming down a trail that curved around the base of a mountain. Where the trail began to turn right was a very pretty meadow filled with blueberry bushes. In that meadow was a young grizzly bear **_cub_**, enjoying the sunshine and a delightful brunch.

I felt three quarts of blood drain from my body.

If you see a grizzly bear cub it means the mother—the very large, angry mother, of that youngster is somewhere looking at you while she contemplates how much of your remains to store in her den for leisurely winter snacking.

My brother and I froze and barely took a breath for what seemed like forever. Then, I got one of the greatest ideas I have ever had.

I slowly bent down on one knee and began tightening the laces on my hiking boots.

Bewildered that I would risk moving at all, he said, "What are you doing?"

My reply was simple, rational, and justifiably self-interested.

"If that mother bear comes out of there, I am getting the hell out of here."

He then reminded me that I had not listened to the part of the park ranger's talk when he said, "No human can outrun a grizzly bear."

Glancing up at my younger, and only, brother, I bluntly replied, "No, but I can outrun **_you_**."

His expression was one of, "That is correct, but surely he wouldn't. . . ."

Fortunately, I did not have to resort to my Jesse Owens impersonation while my brother became lunch. Mama bear never came out, and many minutes later we snuck out of there, got to the car, and have not brought up traveling together in the wilderness again.

To this day, his account of these events differs from mine. I remind him of how, when he was a boy, he went out on a camping trip and ended up covered in ticks. The resulting fever probably deteriorated his ability to accurately remember things that are all his fault.

Speaking of things that are other people's fault . . .

One fall I traveled to Smoky Mountain National Park with Sarah and our boys along with two other families. Sarah—always the considerate one—thought it would be fun to invite these couples that had somewhere between 9 and 15 kids, combined (I lost count) to join us.

I am always reluctant to have people camp with us because as any tent camper knows, once you get your systems in place, adding other annoyances—like humans—messes up your system. On top of that is the fact that when you invite other people along, good intentions can go south quickly.

She also thought it would be a great idea to bring along two wonderful children's books—*Every Autumn Comes the Bear* and *Owl Moon*—to read to all the kids around the campfire, because as everyone surely knows, all campfires should have animal stories.

What she did not know was that some of the youngsters were deathly afraid of everything from moths to Nile Crocodiles. She also did not know that the mother of those children had not spent much of her life in the woods but probably a great deal of it shopping at urban malls.

The wonderful thing about Mrs. Chambless is that when she thinks something is a great idea, she proceeds under the assumption that everyone else will come around to seeing it the same way.

Nope.

The first night we were there, with about three basketball teams' worth of youngsters sitting by the campfire, my lovely bride pulled out these books and began reading them with all the drama one would expect from campfire tales.

Out there in the cosmos, someone decided it was time to traumatize these already trembling kids.

Not one second after she finished reading, a large coyote appeared at our campsite, standing on a small hill looking down at all of us. The shadow he cast made him look like a giant, kid-hunting wild dog.

The little girls of the mom who had never been in the wild screamed and took off running. As they were running, as God is my witness, a large owl came swooping out of a tree and did a military jet flyover inches above the heads of these panicked—and fleeing—youngsters.

The crying and wailing lasted well into the night.

The following day, we all decided to take a hike along a well-traveled trail where you are more likely to run across people in sandals and ironed shirts than any four-legged creatures.

We all made it up to the typical touristy waterfall in short order and began forming up to take our required "look at us" photo when I heard some commotion around a bend.

Sure enough, just as my wife's book selection predicted, it was autumn and there was a bear.

This little guy was sitting maybe fifteen yards off the trail and appeared to be one of those bears that idiots feed when they are taking thirty minutes away from Gatlinburg, Tennessee, to "rough it." There were maybe forty people gathered around taking photos, waving, calling out to him, and generally acting like morons.

The little girls that had freaked completely out the night before had just walked up when the bear decided to get a little closer to the donut-wielding guests.

The screaming and running this created were even louder and faster than the owl and coyote festival from the night before.

Making matters worse, the children we were camping with were joined by adults who were screaming and running too. I have never been to Spain to see the running of the bulls, but this sufficed.

The next day, the family with the terrorized children packed up and left. To my knowledge they never set foot in the woods again, sleep with the lights on, and only walk in malls.

I am just glad they were not around when we met Marvin the moose.

As hard to believe as this might be—the experts on wild animals that live near campgrounds and hiking trails seem to believe that moose are far more dangerous animals than bears in many instances.

The problem with this reality is that at the turn of the century the internet was not yet full of videos, social media postings, and valuable animal attack data, so when I took my family on a hike in Grand Teton National Park (ca. 2005) we were under the impression that moose were similar to cows, but with longer legs and antlers.

Halfway into the hike I decided to stretch out in a patch of grass to close my eyes for a minute.

When you are a parent of very young children you do not get to close your eyes for a minute.

"Dad, look—a moose!" I heard from Gabriel, our four-year old at the time.

Knowing he was kind of a miniature jokester I offered up some exaggerated threat to anyone disturbing my attempt to nap, but he persisted until I sat up, and lo and behold, there was a moose standing near a pond close by.

Since I have a home in Florida and I am a man, naturally a "Florida-man" decision was made to get up, get my camera, and follow this moose.

He led me to a larger pond at the edge of the woods—and off the designated hiking trail—where I proceeded to get some wonderful photos of this guy. Heck, he even turned his head to look at me with lily pads and water dripping from his mouth. It was as if he knew I was friendly and therefore he was cooperating with my photographic pursuits.

Not really . . .

Slowly, he turned and began coming out of the pond. Out of the corner of my eye I saw another moose come out of the willows and join "Marvin" (the name I had given my new wilderness friend).

Together, they proceeded to walk in the direction of me, my family, and two other hikers who thought seeing moose in the wild, up close, was a temporary good idea.

Lunch interrupted

As if they were NFL pulling guards escorting a running back down the sidelines, these irritated ungulates kept all of us bunched up along the shoreline as they escorted us out of the woods, back on the trail, off the trail, into the parking lot, in our cars and out of their sight.

Apparently, as Google would later teach us, we were all kind of close to getting drop-kicked and frequently stepped on by Marvin and his cousin.

Wyoming, with the smallest human population in the US, is, for some reason, *the* state to encounter the largest numbers of four-legged individuals with very precise views on property rights and how to enforce those rights.

One morning, somewhere around one minute after the sun had come up, I heard a loud swooshing sound right outside the tent that I did not put up.

Trying to get more sleep all I could think was, "What the hell is that sound??!"

So, in my normal reaction to irritating circumstances, I hastily scrambled to the zipper of the door to our tent, grabbed it, and abruptly opened the very thin, very unprotective door.

Somewhere between 7 and 7.25 inches away was a male bison with a head the size of a Volkswagen.

The swooshing sound was him moving his head side to side to get to the lush grass that he wanted in front of my door.

He paused for a couple of seconds and slowly looked right into my eyes with an expression that said something like, "Good morning. I weigh a couple of tons and need to eat this grass. Trampling you into sawdust would not be an unreasonable act if you do not go back into that little house."

The zipper slowly closed and not a peep was made until he had turned around and headed back toward Idaho.

While you will not run into bison or grizzly bears in the forests and lakes of Minnesota, you are still not immune from unusual—and potentially painful—animal encounters.

The first thing people think of, I would assume, as they consider venturing into the Land of Ten Thousand Lakes, is that very large, non-domesticated dogs live there.

According to the folks that conduct a census for wolves, there are around 2,700 of these glorious animals roaming the state.

Timberwolf near Ely, Minnesota (January 2007)

Inasmuch as there are zero documented cases of wolves attacking human beings anywhere in the state of Minnesota, I would suggest that the census takers help those of us who camp in this beautiful part of the country by counting snapping turtles instead.

When glaciers receded after the last Ice Age and carved out the pristine lakes of this state, somehow large, trash-can lid sized turtles with iron clamps for jaws decided to move in.

And they do not care about your size relative to theirs.

One afternoon in 2015 I was fishing (it is a requirement for camping in Minnesota) off a large rock near our Crab Lake campsite when I felt something very odd happening on my foot.

A second later, I realized that the feeling was coming from an enormous, prehistoric snapping turtle positioning himself for a free meal.

The force of his top jaw snapping onto the top of my toes was something akin to a jackhammer that is used to break up concrete—or so I am guessing.

If not for the fact that I never, even on the beaches of Florida, walk around bare foot (I put on some form of shoes the moment I get out of bed), I would be known as Jack, the seven-toed Florida Man. He was simply unable to get his bottom jaw under my foot because of my sandals.

The backflip I did on that rock caused the 3,000-year-old reptile to leap back into the water and recalibrate his dinner plans for the first person in our group to take an evening swim.

Meanwhile, at night in the north woods of Minnesota you will often hear the awe-inspiring, and prolonged howls of wolves—and none of them try to bite your feet while you are there.

Wildlife tips

Every good tent camper knows that animals are everywhere, and they do not subscribe to the idea that we are in charge, or that we have dominion over their habitat. They also seem to know that humans are generally stupid and selfish, and they do not care about that either.

Choosing the vacation lifestyle of tent camping requires you to follow some basic, common-sense rules.

First, in bear territory, take a strong rope and tie it to the end of your food pack. Then, take a rock or some other heavy item and tie it to the other end of the rope. Throw the rock over a large limb that is far away from the trunk of the tree, let gravity bring the rock to you, then proceed to tie the rope off after you have raised your food pack well off the ground and well away from the tree trunk. Do this many, many, many yards away from your campsite.

DO NOT discard food in your firepit or in the bushes nearby.

DO NOT sleep in the clothes you cook or eat in.

DO NOT leave any dirty dishes or anything that smells—deodorant, toothpaste, anything—in your tent. All of that should go in the secure food pack.

Second, the wilderness is not a petting zoo. Before you leave on your camping trip go online and read about the animals who make their homes where you are going. Learn what to do if you come across a mountain lion or a mountain goat. Memorize these instructions and NEVER approach or attempt to feed any wildlife.

Their diet does not include the junk we eat, and they are not sitting there hoping for visitors. Well, maybe grizzly bears have this hope, but not many of the others.

Third, read the warning signs on designated trails.

Speaking of reading signs, in 2022 Sarah and I were hiking part of the Appalachian Trail in north Georgia. Stupidly, we walked right by a sign—that we later saw while slowing down from running—that warned of black bears and snakes on the trail. This is a seemingly odd combination, but someone in Georgia knows what they are talking about.

A couple of miles into our hike we were leaving a scenic overlook where we had been admiring Georgia's early fall colors, when our dog Jake came within three feet of stepping on an enormous Timber Rattlesnake that was slowly making its way past the trail that he did not know was reserved for human beings.

Only a few seconds after we left the snake, I looked up into a tall tree up ahead and said, "Hey, look. A bear."

Sarah thought I was playing a mean joke on her to take advantage of her already frazzled nerves until she looked up in time to see a small black bear cub shimmying down the tree ahead of his mother who was right behind him.

The rattlesnake must have been startled as Sarah and Jake soared past him.

Panting in the parking lot, I looked up at the trail entrance information board and said, "Hey look, they have a bear and snake warning up there."

2

Camping with—and Anywhere Near—Humans

Growing up in the rural town of Hugo, Oklahoma, it was not unheard of for kids to venture out for a night or two of tent camping even before they had reached their teenage years.

For me, this meant first pitching a tent in the large field near our home for my twelfth and thirteenth birthday celebrations.

Each year, I would round up a few friends and we would walk to the local convenience store to load up on junk food. This store would have sold us beer and cigarettes too, but we were not yet interested in that kind of lifestyle.

My go-to food and beverage were a king-size bag of nacho cheese Doritos and a six-pack of Peach Nehi. I would then stay up all night long talking about girls, sports, and other middle-school topics, only interrupted by walks all over our deserted little town, while drinking 96 ounces of Nehi and consuming every crumb of MSG-laden chips. The splitting headache the next morning was a natural byproduct of these dietary choices and zero minutes of sleep.

It should be noted that at no time did any parents show up at our campsite to check on us. That would have interrupted *Gunsmoke, Kojak,* or some other adult programming and would have required worrying about teenage boys at a level that was rare in the late 1970s. I do not recall ever hearing, "So, how was the camping?" And, of course, since cell phones had not been invented no one ever texted us or tracked us as we ventured out at 2 a.m. to walk around town. Heck, I don't even think I told my parents about the night I saw a ghost that was the exact height and shape of R2D2 from *Star Wars* hanging out in our pasture.

A few years later, my high school camping trips of choice were split between two groups of friends. The first was made up of guys I played high school football with. Every fall we would get one Friday night off and would use it to head for the Ouachita Mountains.

Our trips to the mountains yielded some of the most memorable times of my youth, especially in 1983 when we landed on the question of "What do you think you will be doing in the year 2000?" while we were gathered around a good fire.

When you are seventeen the thought of being thirty-four is ludicrous. Moreover, when you are tent camping during the height of the Cold War you take it seriously when one of your campmates says, "Why are we talking about 2000?—we won't even be here by then." That comment came right around the time ABC released the made-for-television movie, *The Day After*, which depicted life near Kansas City after the beginning of World War III. I recall that it was a quiet, somber, and reflective moment for me and my friends. It also did not help much that months later, Hollywood came out with *Red Dawn* which had every teenager in America wondering if you could really go camping and simultaneously fight the Soviet Union.

My second group of tent camping friends—a group that seemed to change quite often—would travel with me to the outskirts of town near an abandoned domicile known as the Chumley House.

The Chumley House, even in the daytime, was frightening and most assuredly haunted by whomever Chumley was. No real story about ghosts ever got around about this place but everyone in town knew something eerie and bad lurked around the grounds and both levels of this once proud home.

Camping a hundred yards or so in front of this house, far from our parents, was a test of our courage. We would challenge one another to walk up to the house alone and would enjoy fires with the silhouette of this scary place looming nearby. That is, until the night the Prince of Darkness appeared.

I have a lifelong friend, Kirk Butler, who joined me one night out at Mr. Chumley's place. It was the first time Kirk had camped there and, as he told me forty-two years later, it was his last.

Earlier in our high school years Kirk had become an evangelical Christian which must have come in handy while he was sitting with us by the campfire. I noticed that he had grown suspiciously silent and was just staring at the ground with a somewhat concerned expression on his face.

This must have gone on for a few minutes until I looked over at him and asked, "Kirk, what is the matter?"

His response is the reason why I still claim to this day to be the world-record holder in the 100-meter dash.

"Guys, I don't know, but I think the devil is out here with us," was his measured answer.

At that precise moment, for no reason other than Satan actually being there, a huge rush of wind came up through the campfire, from the coals to the top, and caused the fire to instantly, and loudly, grow by several feet!

I know that Usain Bolt once covered 100 meters in 9.58 seconds. His feat was on television and recorded electronically.

On that chilly fall evening in Oklahoma, I am quite certain that I ran a wind- and Satan-aided first 100 meters in around 6.91 seconds. My second 100 meters, as I kept running toward town, was slightly slower, maybe 8.27 seconds.

For all I know, my sleeping bag is still lying out in front of the Chumley House.

But at least Satan did not try to drown me . . .

In June of 1984, I was a new graduate of Hugo High School.

Enjoying one more summer of freedom meant, of course, getting a tent and finding a friend to head to the woods.

Reb Bowers was, like me, about to head off to college to play baseball. He had just won the class 3A high school batting title in Oklahoma and was looking forward to his next athletic challenge.

He did not count on this challenge involving swimming in rapids to save his own life—and that of a third grader.

Our college baseball coaches did not know that they almost lost us to a blend of stupidity, bad hearing, and one screaming little kid who ironically was named Rocky.

Our camping destination is a true natural wonder of Oklahoma—Beavers Bend State Park. If you have never been to the Sooner State, this is a jewel to stop at no matter what your vacation plans are.

The lake in this state park, like others in my home state, was created by the construction of a dam that is used to generate electricity.

Along one particular trail in this park you will see very large, very clear signs in the English language that warn people about the dangers of swimming in this area.

The reason is simple. Every time a loud horn is sounded, the dam is opened, millions of gallons of water are released, and a smaller version of Niagara Falls come pouring over the spillway with incredible force.

Thus, if you are down river when this tsunami appears you can get swept away by the rushing current and end up not playing college baseball.

As seventeen-year-old males, ignoring the signs was step one. Going down below the spillway to swim was step two.

Step three was me telling my friend and his young family friend, who happened to be camping nearby and asked if he could join us at the river, that I was a trained lifeguard, so we should be fine. It was true that I had been a lifeguard at a city pool for two years. It was not true that we would be fine.

During our revelry swimming in the Mountain Fork River, we did not hear the sirens blaring out the warning that we were about to be under water.

One of us happened to look up—in the direction of the spillway—and noticed that the people who ran this dam were not joking.

As the torrent of water came over the spillway and the water began to fill the river rapidly, the little dude with us came completely unhinged. Perhaps it was the fact that the only land we could find was rapidly disappearing below our feet.

Maybe it was the current that looked like the Colorado River going through the Grand Canyon. Whatever it was, this little eight-year-old knew somehow that he had picked idiots to hang out with that day.

With what was likely a minute or two to spare, the only lifeguard in the group decided to swim up ahead to find a way out of this disaster. As soon as

Mountain Fork Spillway, Beavers Bend State Park—37 years later

I got in the water, I knew I was going to likely make the shore somewhere in Kentucky.

After I finally fought the current long enough to make it to land, my buddy put the panicked youngster on his back and stepped off our little island and into the raging river.

With this fellow choking him every inch of the way and screaming like a banshee in both of his ears, he swam as hard as he possibly could toward the bank where I was waving him in. Reb thought for sure that the little kid might drown him, but he eventually made it and collapsed on the ground with Rocky (far from Balboa) still crying.

Nearly four decades later, my friend and I visited this spot while staying at Beavers Bend Lodge with our wives.

After showing them the spillway, where we were swimming back in 1984, where we ended up and how we ended up there, both ladies muttered something along the lines of, "Boy, are you two stupid."

Well said.

Unfortunately, like many other males, getting older has not eliminated my ability to make stupid decisions from time to time.

In the summer of 1998 Sarah and I took our very first camping trip. We had a hand-me-down tent with duct tape repairs all over it and some cheap yoga mats for a mattress.

We had not yet learned anything about air mattresses so even though she was a few months pregnant with our first son, she was all for toughing it out the way pioneers did in 1898.

I must admit, her pregnancy came in handy many times when we would get to a camping area that did not have any remaining sites. From the Oregon coast to a campground near (way too near) the Seatac Airport in Seattle, "My young wife is pregnant and needs a place to rest" was a fantastic calling card to get a campground host to say, "You can pitch your tent right over there . . ."

So, this is exactly what we did one evening after a long day of hiking near Mt. St. Helens, in Washington.

Extremely tired and hungry, we came upon a park ranger who informed us that we could camp in undesignated sites off the main road, and outside the borders of the national monument.

So, after a good bit of searching for the right spot—far from any signs of humans—we came across a beautiful location on top of an overlook. It was tucked down behind some large rocks and gave us panoramic views of the wilderness around Mt. St. Helens.

It also gave us the closest call we have ever had in our nearly thirty years in the woods.

That evening, we had just finished a wonderful dinner of trout with blueberry and cornbread stuffing my wife invented and were settling in by a nice campfire. The bonus was a full moon and cloudless sky that made the stars seem like they were only feet away.

With no outhouse or other modern conveniences nearby, I stepped away from camp to relieve myself. I walked up on some boulders near the old dirt logging road we had come in on to set up our camp.

The full moon was behind me so I could see the large moonlit hillside across the road as clear as day.

As I surveyed the landscape, I was shocked to see two human beings walking from my right to left on top of the hill. It was very late so the idea of someone still day hiking did not make sense. But the last thing I wanted was for some hikers to accidentally come up to our camp, so I decided to call out to them—as a courtesy—to let them know there was a camper down the hill from them.

That was almost one of the biggest mistakes of my entire life.

"Hey there, I don't mean to alarm you, but I am camping nearby and just wanted to let you know so you do not accidentally come up on our camp."

At that precise moment, the two figures, which were about twenty yards apart, stopped. Then, the one in front turned and slowly walked back to his partner where both stood and stared down the hill in my direction.

What happened next was a near catastrophe.

They separated and then started walking *down the hill* toward our camp!

To this day I get the same chills thinking about this moment in my life as I did when it happened.

I was, for obvious reasons, in complete shock and disbelief over what I was seeing. I am also willing to admit that I was scared out of my mind.

Standing on that boulder I felt my legs begin to shake violently.

Here I was, miles from anywhere in the middle of the night with my young pregnant wife back at camp, oblivious to what was happening, and I had two lunatics coming down a hill to do God-knows-what.

I decided to use reasoning one more time. I thought maybe they did not clearly hear me the first time I called out, so I tried again.

"Hey, if you are out hiking and need something to eat or drink that is fine but let me know."

They stopped for ten to fifteen seconds upon hearing this declaration.

Not uttering a sound, they continued to very slowly zigzag down the steep grade toward the road and in my direction, stopping briefly behind trees from time to time. I had no idea if they could see me but at this point it did not matter.

Within seconds, my sheer terror turned to volcanic anger and the expletive-heavy threats came out loud and with great frequency.

"I can see both of you! I am armed and I will #$&^@! shoot both of you if you do not get out of here right now!"*

Once again, they paused momentarily, did not say a word, and then kept coming.

By now Sarah had heard the commotion and peeked out behind the rocks we were camping behind.

I shouted, "Kevin, bring me my gun." My wife's first, middle, or nickname is not Kevin but the last thing I wanted to make known was that a female was nearby.

Either brilliantly, or ridiculously, depending on your perspective, I whispered to her to break down camp as fast as she could and let me know when she was done.

This is, to this day, a subject of great debate in our household when this trip comes up for discussion. She maintains that we should have just left camp—even if it meant everything would be stolen—and just get out of there. She is almost 100 percent correct in this after-the-fact assessment of what could have happened to us.

I remind her that these two maniacs were still 200–300 hundred yards away, I did have protection and that in 1998 we did not have much money. A completely destroyed or stolen camp would have meant going home to Florida with only the clothes on our backs and where there are even more criminals walking around than in the woods of Washington. And there was one more thing . . .

Somehow the thought of being chased out of there AND having our property stolen was infuriating enough to make me think that they might send us packing but they would gain nothing else that night.

As the seconds went by and the two invaders crept closer, my warnings grew louder and the threats more severe.

As they paused at one point, I told myself that if they made it to the ditch next to the logging road (about fifty yards from where I was standing), that I was going to leave the rock, walk in their direction and then let the National Park Service and local authorities determine what the word "justifiable" means.

At that critical point I saw my wife wave for me. She had packed what sparse camping gear we had with incredible speed and handed me the keys.

I do not know if those guys ever made it to the ditch. I do know that we got out of there as fast as we could, looking in our rearview mirror for any sign of them. We have also avoided old logging roads in the middle of nowhere since then.

We drove (quickly) to the nearest designated campground and found our-selves uncharacteristically disappointed to find it empty. This was one night when a campground filled with people would have been preferable—given our frayed nerves and a newfound belief that there may be safety in numbers. However, it was very late, and we were spent, so we set up camp while looking over our shoulders.

As we attempted to sleep, some deranged squirrels (or escaped convicts) kept dropping sticks and other projectiles on our tent which left us jumping and twitching all night long.

As unnerving as that incident was, over the years, I have discovered that it is not always hiking derelicts creeping toward your tent that create major problems.

Sometimes when you leave the comforts of your campsite, even for just a little while in civilization, disaster can find you.

October 20, 2004, should have been one of the great days of my life. That is the day that the Boston Red Sox—the team I have rooted for since 1978—were on the precipice of one of the greatest comebacks in sports history.

Just one year earlier we were camping at the Cosby Campground in the Smoky Mountain National Park where, in violation of my policies about bringing civilization camping, I toted along a small radio to listen to the 2003 American League Championship Series.

The year 2003, for you baseball fans, is the year Boston lost to the Yankees after some arguably poor managing and untimely hitting ended the Red Sox season.

In 2004 we were back at Cosby and my team was getting wiped out again.

Then, a miracle happened. After falling behind 3 games to none, Boston won games 4, 5 and 6, setting up the historic game 7 match.

Baseball games start late and end late, so I informed Mrs. Chambless that after she and the boys went to sleep, I was going to drive down about a mile to this little bar at the bottom of an old country store and watch game 7. She understood what game 7 meant and the boys were already dozing off.

So off I went . . .

When I walked into that little bar, which had only two or three tables, a large confederate flag and assorted offerings of moonshine, I heard a loud, gruff, and somewhat unsettling voice boom out, "I'll take this one!"

As I glanced in the direction of where this declaration had come from, I saw a very large woman with around 5 teeth (mostly black ones) smiling at me as if I was the first offering at the Golden Corral.

It was tempting to run back to my tent and leave my car there. I was even missing the two crazy people from Mt. St. Helens.

But, by golly, this was GAME 7 and so I slowly nodded and kept walking a few more feet to the bar.

Somewhere around three seconds after Johnny Damon hit a grand-slam home run into the upper deck, my wild cheering and clapping was interrupted by the man sitting with the woman who had her eyes set on me.

"*Whare you frum, boy?*" was his question.

"Florida."

"*Well whet tha hell you a-doin up in these parts?*"

"I am tent camping with my family nearby and came down to watch the ballgame."

"*You mean you a-sittin here watchin baseball whilst yer family is some-wheres else?*"

"Yes, but they don't care. They are asleep."

"*Well, you sorry* ____, *I ough-ta* _______________."

Note—I am not sure how to fill in the previous blanks since he was drunk, and backwoods Tennessee profanity is hard for most people to understand.

As he stood up to continue his threats over my decision to watch a baseball game in the United States of America as a free human being, the woman with him stood up too.

Now the thought crossed my mind that I was about to be violated by one hillbilly and one hillbillyette.

Recalling the only time in my life I have ever watched the movie *Deliverance*, I calmly put my right hand in the air, waved at this moonshine consuming gentlemen and said something along the lines of, "You know, I never thought of it that way. I think you are right."

I listened to the rest of the game on my cheap little radio, the Red Sox made it to the World Series, and all night I had dreams that I was being chased from Mt. St. Helens to Tennessee by a band of miscreants.

3

Rain, Lightning, and 108 MPH Winds

I would guess that for most people the idea of camping in a tent—even if the biggest animal you see is a ground squirrel and the humans near you are kind and law-abiding—is less than desirable because of the unknown variability of the weather.

I learned, from an early age, that bad weather follows people with tents. It appears to be someone's way of saying, "If you are stupid enough to pick camping over a real roof and indoor plumbing, try *this* on for size!"

Not more than a year after my daredevil spill and stitches, I found myself standing next to my mother and little brother as we all tried to hold up our tent at Lake Texoma that was trying to blow over because of a tornado nearby. My mother had managed, on an earlier camping trip, to pick up a six-pack of Dr. Pepper, see a live Copperhead snake (yes, they are poisonous) wrapped around the handle, and gently set it down without screaming.

The tornado had her screaming.

We were failing miserably at keeping this tent from caving in or carrying all of us to Kansas, as my father, who had been out bowfishing, pulled up and laughed hysterically at our efforts. My German mother called him, and this tent camping fiasco, things in German that probably cannot be repeated, and she swore she would never go back to Lake Texoma (she hasn't).

I hate camping in the rain and bad weather too. I have had many trips that have resembled life in the Amazon. One day of being in a tent in the rain is a great day to relax, take several naps, and get caught up on a good book.

Two or sixteen days in a row is disgusting—especially if your tent leaks and/or the wind picks up as the temperatures fall.

I do not recall what Noah made the Ark out of, but I know it was not polyester. I also know what the word "waterproof" is supposed to mean. But that word is a load of ostrich dung when it comes to tents. There is, in my experience, no such thing as a waterproof tent. There is only, "water *resistant* until it lets the water in."

Case in point:

In 2013 my family and I ventured into the Canadian Maritimes to enjoy some of the most beautiful scenery and friendliest people anywhere on Earth.

If you are a tent camper, or aspire to be one, put Nova Scotia, New Brunswick, and Newfoundland at, or near, the top of your list of destinations.

But first, spend $179 on a new rain jacket and buy lots and lots of tarps, rope, and small shovels (to dig miniature Panama Canals away from your tent).

Go ahead and use the spray that is supposed to waterproof your tent. But you might as well use a can of furniture polish.

On our first trip to Nova Scotia, we did not have any tarps, shovels, or expensive rain jackets. We had two tents—one for my wife and I and one for our then teenaged sons.

The first day we were in Cape Breton we came across a large group of campers from Lichtenstein. I am guessing, based on the number of tents, that we got to meet around 20 percent of the entire population of that small nation. We also saw tarps—lots of them—on these tents.

That night we wished we were citizens of Lichtenstein.

Being from Florida we are accustomed to severe lightning. But Nova Scotia lightning takes on biblical proportions which caused my wife to break into her *Chicken Run* routine. Oddly, in addition to bouncing up and down and flapping her imaginary wings, my wife also loses the ability to hear. The louder I say, "Please do not panic," the tighter her ears close and the more she panics. This spontaneous deafness during natural weather patterns was on full display with each bolt of lightning.

All she could think of was, "Get out of this tent. Get the boys out of their tent. Get in the car."

OK, here lies a problem. Telling teenage boys to wake up, go out in torrential rain, and get in the car so Mommy and Daddy can drive around until it is safe, is not a way to endear them to you, or get speedy cooperation. But she did it anyway.

Which brings us to problem #2. When we are on long camping trips, over time the inside of our car tends to resemble the combination of a large garbage dump and a hotel room that an entire frat house has visited.

When we all tried to load into our SUV during this apocalyptic storm, there wasn't anywhere to sit comfortably. We had set up camp and planned to clean the car the next day.

So, with all of us piled on top of dirty clothes, trash bags, and other assorted—and disgusting—clutter, we proceeded to drive out of the campground and down a road leading to a scenic vista overlooking the ocean. Yes, it was still dark, we were soaking wet, and we could not see much unless lightning lit up the sky, but hey, at least we were safer, according to my wife.

When the storm appeared to be over, we drove back to camp, crawled back into our tents and were just about to fall asleep when the Maritimes decided to give us more excitement.

In the middle of the first lightning strike, Sarah was gone and back at the boys' tent rousting them out into this new storm. This time I am certain I heard profanity—long profanity—from one or both of my sons. Or maybe it was me. I do not recall.

I do know we were back in the car driving around (she said having rubber tires would save us) until that storm left.

When we got back to camp our sons dove into their tents with mumbled threats about waking them up again.

When I unzipped our tent I noticed, even in the dark, that our mattress was moving in a gentle, sort of bobbing manner.

How to fix a broken tent. . . .

I stepped into the tent to get a better look when I noticed that I was standing in water that was about 4" deep. The mattress was simply floating around like any device with air in it should.

With our non-Lichtenstein preparations causing a destroyed tent and with our sons nearby, we notified them that we would be moving in with them for the foreseeable future.

The next day, my mechanically inclined bride decided she could fix our tent. She is the handyperson of our house and can fix almost anything. So, while she was preparing to make our tent livable again, I did something that I am quite skilled at. I took out the trash.

I hauled the tent to a large dumpster, dragging it along the ground the entire way, and tossed it in. I may have even called it a bad name, but it doesn't matter.

Ten years later, we got our second chance to battle the Canadian Maritimes.

This time, we were ready. Mostly.

The Walmart and Canadian Tire in Sussex, New Brunswick, has camping tarps the size of Rhode Island and lots of rope, shovels, and other, "Let's camp in Canada, eh?" gear.

When we arrived in Fundy National Park, Sarah put up the tents (one for us, one that I use as my personal closet) and then said something brilliant.

"Why don't you take Jake (our Golden Retriever) for a walk?"

I knew exactly what that meant.

One of my flaws is that I sometimes come up with construction-related ideas and say them out loud. At home in Florida when she and my youngest son work on projects together, I offer suggestions. For some reason, every suggestion leads to an invitation for me to go to Ace Hardware to buy a screw or some birdfeed.

So, she knew when I pulled out the tarps and rope, I was going to have an idea of how to waterproof our camp. She also knew that if I helped, the result would look like something out of a *Three Stooges* episode.

An hour or so later I came back to find something that Frank Lloyd Wright could not have pulled off and during the next two weeks of near constant rain, her tarps, rope, and insistence that I do not touch anything, paid off—with one exception.

Smart as she is, it did not dawn on her to tarp the bottom of the tent. So, when the remnants of a hurricane swept through the Maritimes, we awoke to our dog leaping from his bed to our bed to avoid the Mississippi River that was flowing across our floor.

Making matters slightly worse, the day we broke down camp we took this enormous tarp out into the sunshine to shake off the water and attempt to dry

Canadian roof work (ca. 2023)

it out. Sarah had one end of it (I thought) and I had the other. Before she was ready, I began shaking the tarp just as a strong breeze kicked up. This caused it to flap wildly, which sent Sarah running away from the water that was now flying everywhere.

One problem emerged from that decision.

She ran away from the blue plastic roof without noticing the ditch—kind of a steep one—that she was fleeing toward.

From my vantage point all I could see was her arms flailing while she looked back in my direction. Her sprinting form looked much like someone who was intoxicated.

Then she disappeared.

Precisely one-half of my male brain was concerned about my wife taking a tumble into the ditch. The other half thought it was one of the funniest things I had seen in a long time.

When I got to her and asked if she was OK, she said she was unhurt.

I thought I was going to dislocate a rib muscle from laughing so hard.

Laughing while tent camping—even if sometimes it seems inappropriate to do so—is an integral part of dealing with the absurdity that living outdoors delivers.

Case in point.

Journeying into Minnesota's Boundary Waters Canoe Wilderness Area in the summer and then finding your way into the remote lakes that dot this region is just about as close to living like the first humans as you are going to get. This part of the United States is a jewel of our protected lands and waterways.

It is a pristine, quiet, mind-clearing environment that every serious tent camper should pursue at least once in their lifetime.

We have traveled to the BWCA since 2005 and have camped in the back-country many times.

The first time we ever ventured onto canoes and into habitat that wolves thrive in, I found myself standing at the desk of Piragis Outfitters in Ely, Minnesota, discussing the types of packs and gear that were necessary to have a successful trip. At one point, the outfitter helping us said, "After you cross this large lake you will portage your gear through these woods to your next launch site."

Incredibly, I asked out loud, "So, what does portage mean?"

"It means to carry your shit through the woods."

Got it.

My second stupid question was, "So, what do you do when you run out of water?"

We were told that you take a big plastic collapsible jug, paddle your canoe out into a wide expanse in the middle of the lake, lean out of your canoe (without tipping over), and dip the jug as far under the surface as you can to get water. Then, we were told, you take the jug back to camp and put in some sort of water treatment tablets to purify it. All of this is because for some reason beavers tend to fumigate the lakes with something called Giardia which can cause "Beaver Fever."

Getting beaver fever is apparently up there near the bubonic plague so when the outfitter's rep finished telling us how to get fresh water I nodded, said "thank you" and mumbled something along the lines of "Stupid beavers."

When we first started backcountry camping, we learned about an important rule to follow when you are packing your gear. That rule is that "Every ounce matters."

On our first trip, we did not pay attention to this rule. That is because my job is the staging of what I think we need to take. Sarah's job is the actual packing. And, when I was not looking, she packed like we were leaving for a year-long trek across Africa.

If you have ever seen a canoeing backcountry pack you will recall thinking, "Wow, a refrigerator made from some sort of canvas. What will they think of next?"

When you are carrying an engorged canoeing pack through the woods you will think to yourself, "Wow, this is what a *%#$)&!@* refrigerator feels like."

It did not help matters that Sarah, without telling me about it, put the full-size KING JAMES BIBLE in my pack. When I eventually discovered what she had done I said things that, if there is a hell, will get me elected hell's mayor upon my arrival.

That first trip featured one long, four-person Kevlar canoe with Sarah, our then seven- and five-year-old boys and me. Of course, our two massive packs were crammed in there too along with fishing gear and everything else we could think of. How we did not flip over on the way to the Crab Lake portage is beyond me.

How canoeing novices travel

After paddling across Burntside Lake—a huge and confusing expanse—we finally found the portage trail.

I knew that Sarah would take care of our boys along the trail while carrying one portage pack. My job was to carry the other pack—and canoe—along a path that had huge rocks, roots, deep mud, and uneven terrain.

This is my way of making an excuse for what happened next.

To theoretically save time, I had the brilliant idea that I would put our personal refrigerator—and the hidden Bible inside it—on my back and then put the canoe on my shoulders to portage both at the same time.

There was only one, or seventeen, potential problems with this plan.

The first problem was one of physics. Carrying that much weight on my back while trying to semi-blindly navigate a trail with a 23-foot long, 64 lb.

four-person canoe on my shoulders would possibly lead to weight and volume distribution issues.

Sarah and the boys had already taken off ahead of me when, with the help of two other campers, I hoisted the pack and then the canoe.

Only a minute or so up the trail the canoe got stuck on my head, shoulders, and canoe pack and I completely freaked out.

I swear, I do not know how the hell turtles live in shells without going insane.

I then made another mistake by letting my claustrophobia cause me to start running up the trail. I could barely see and just knew that someone was going to have to cut this canoe off my head, which made me combine shouting with running.

Sarah turned around to see me sprinting blindly and begging, loudly, "Get it off me! Get it off me!"

This caused her to do what every concerned wife would do.

She laughed until her bladder began to give way.

When I realized that I was on my own I stopped, grabbed the canoe and with everything I had in me, wrestled it off my back and flung it over the trail and into the bushes.

She continued laughing all the way up the trail.

She was still laughing when she bent over to help our five-year–old go to the bathroom. The weight of her pack shifted just enough to make her lose her balance and fall on him. He was lying under his mother and her prehistoric size turtle shell pack as she struggled to get back on her feet. It took both boys to get her upright. Again, I do not know how turtles do this.

She was still laughing at me as I dropped off the first pack, went back for the canoe, and brought it back to Crab Lake. She laughed as we canoed Crab Lake looking for a campsite and she laughed while we set up camp.

In 2024 when I got my foot stuck—twice—in our youngest son's whitewater raft she laughed and reminded me of the canoe that was stuck on my head nineteen years earlier.

As the years and our trips to Minnesota went by, we became something akin to experts in backcountry canoe camping.

Except for one thing.

What to do in a lightning storm when it is impossible to get to your car.

This was the question Mrs. *Chicken Run* asked the outfitter in Ely before our 2016 trip.

We had heard there might be some days of storms around July 4, so she wanted to find out what to do if you are out there with no rubber car tires to protect you.

The answer—something about curling into a ball, crouching down, and getting on your tip toes—seemed anatomically impossible so I did not pay attention to that answer.

Instead, I relied on my age-old go to question of "What is the probability of ______________ happening?" I do this a lot and Sarah never buys it.

On July 4, 2016, someone up there decided that the probability was 100 percent.

July 4, 2016—only a few hours left to smile and enjoy the day

My sons—now seventeen and fifteen—had set their tent up on a high rocky outcrop near a tall tree on the edge of our campsite at Crab Lake. Being normal teenage boys—and remembering Nova Scotia—they wanted to be as far from us as possible.

Sarah and I were on much lower ground and away from larger trees—and a decent distance from our sons.

Late that evening we began to hear rumbling in the distance. At first it sounded exactly like the scene from *Jurassic Park* when the Tyrannosaurus Rex began to make the ground shake.

"What was that?" she asked.

"I think it is fireworks off in the distance" was the best "Oh God, she is about to panic" answer I could think of.

The next flash and round of thunder helped her realize that this was not fireworks. This was the Maritimes all over again with no protection in sight.

As the storm and the intensity of it grew closer and larger I started to foolishly say, "Sarah, don't panic." By her own admission, as she sat cross-legged and began bouncing up and down, her arms began to flail with such intensity that she gained flight for a second or two.

Then, she burst out of the tent, ran—you guessed it—straight to our boys and demanded they pull up their tent and head to lower ground.

They both knew that she was coming, and they tried to argue about her plan. But they eventually relented, pulled up the stakes, and began following her.

So, in the blinding rain, lightning, and very dark forest, the four of us carried their tent and our sleeping bags while our dog Jake stared at us with a "You have got to be kidding me" expression.

Deeper and somewhat lower into the woods we found the spot she wanted.

We set up this soaked (inside and out) tent on what amounted to a little minefield of tree stumps. The five of us crawled in and sat there—wet, cold, and angry. I think I even heard Jake utter an F-bomb while we stared at one another.

Most of the stares/glares were reserved for Sarah. Especially when she sheepishly smiled and said something along the lines of, "Isn't this cozy?"

After an hour or so of shivering in this little dell the storm mercifully ended. Or so we thought.

The boys stayed in their tent on top of the tree stumps while I went back to our other tent where we had originally set up. Sarah, meanwhile, went to the pit toilet in the woods.

Then, fittingly, more exciting Minnesota summer weather arrived.

As the rains and lightning descended upon us, the boys and I realized that the only person not in a tent was their mother and my wife. In the darkness she had become disoriented in the woods.

We could hear her looking for us, but none of us—not even our dog—uttered a word of assistance. The boys thought, "Great, she is going to find Dad." I thought, "Great, she is going to find the boys."

You see, sometimes tent camping requires that we go back to basic survival instincts rather than applying love, benevolence, or a sense of morality to all situations.

This is another way of saying that we hoped she would stay lost in the woods until the storm subsided. . . .

The next day, as we left the Boundary Waters behind, I recall thinking two things.

The first thought was, "I will never go into the backcountry with Sarah again."

The second thought was, "Thank God the winds were not blowing like that night in Tennessee."

One of the most important personal requirements of tent camping is that you and/or the person with equal say in your household must be particularly skilled at not spending money.

That means that when you think of staying in a hotel, motel, Airbnb, or whatever, you have the mindset that the price should be not much more than what Motel 6 charged in 1962. That price was, of course, $6.

For putting a tent on some dirt, $6 is about right.

It is with that in mind that I take you back to October 2006 when a friend of mine (call him Jeff) and I were having a serious conversation about how to deal with a weather report we had just accidentally overheard.

We were walking along in our campground (as usual, Cosby) in the Smoky Mountain National Park when we came upon an older man listening to his radio. We heard something about 50–60 mph wind gusts for this region and began to think about making other arrangements for the night.

I do not remember the name of the motel we passed coming into Cosby, but I am certain it cost more than $6 per night.

For both of us, the thought of breaking down camp (never any fun) at night, on the off chance of encountering winds that are normal during thunderstorms in Florida, was not a pleasant one.

We had already spent the day on top of Max Patch—a stunning mountaintop in North Carolina—playing pickup football in driving sleet and rain and were not in the mood for any more physical activity.

So, as we got back to camp, he explained to his wife and six kids that it might get a bit windy that night as I explained to my wife and kids that I was tired and ready for bed.

To this day I would like to find the weather forecaster who said 50–60 mph winds were likely. I would like to ask them how you get paid for being so wrong.

Somewhere around 8 or 9 in the evening we began hearing what quite literally sounded like twenty 747 jets taking off, side by side. The roaring sound would begin hundreds of yards away and build to a crescendo until it was right on top of the campground. This wind was, according to the National Park Service, just slightly greater than 50 or 60 miles per hour. As it turns out, the winds peaked at *108 miles per hour*—and stayed that way for hours.

Now might be a good place to mention that at that time in our marriage my wife was a deeply religious woman (remember the King James bible packed for the Boundary Waters?) and, in my estimation, a person who reminded everyone of Mary Poppins.

Therefore, in my convoluted way of doing probability theory during emergencies, I concluded that there was no way God will let anything happen to me (not a very good person) if I was right next to her (a great person), at all times.

As the straight-line winds roared through our campground you could see the trees bend in the shape of a small case "n." When they were under the full force of this mountain hurricane they would shake, strain, and contort until the winds passed. Of course, many of them could not withstand this kind of wind so many trees—one million according to the park service—snapped and crashed into the forest around us.

Assured that I had the spiritual insurance of my wife to cover me, I managed to sleep most of the night.

In the tent near us, the wife of the man who is just as cheap as me, kept praying and jumping every time a limb fell from the sky.

The next morning, I emerged from our tent before anyone else. As I walked outside my first thought was that my wife was going to leave me and find the most expensive hotel she could stay in while she planned out the rest of her life without me.

That is because all around us—inches from our tent, our cars, and our kids—were giant trees lying on the ground.

The day before when our wives discussed what we could do if it got exceptionally windy, one of them mentioned huddling in the bathroom. That was a worse idea than not going to a motel because the day after the storm the bathroom was crushed.

An unsafe bathroom—Cosby Campground (October 2006)

The look on the faces of our wives suggested that rather than being mad at the bad weather forecasters, their husbands were to blame.

It was almost as if they thought that somehow our motel-avoidance had caused the winds to be much worse than if we had driven away to safety. The wife of my friend went so far as to say, "Every time we go camping with the Chambless family something like this happens."

I responded to her comment, and these looks that were a mixture of hostility and bewilderment with a simple, logical statement along the lines of, "Wow, that was close." As usual, no one found my perspective useful or amusing.

I should mention that a year or two later we were back in the Smokies in October when a wind of about 30 miles per hour kicked up for a minute or two.

I got my family to a motel so fast it would have made your head spin—and the motel charged more than $6. . . .

Weather Tips—and Things to Do and Not Do

In many parts of North America once a storm system has rolled through you are in the clear.

Everywhere just under the US–Canadian border—and all of eastern Canada—you can never count on just one system coming through. In that part of the world the torrents of rain and accompanying lightning just circle back around as you are drying yourself from the last one.

The year before our July 4 excitement, one day we ventured out several Boundary Waters portages past Angleworm Lake. The boys had canoed far ahead of us and were fishing on the shoreline of another lake. Sarah and I looked up ahead in the distance and saw Gabriel throwing his fishing rod down on a boulder and flailing his arms around wildly.

"What's wrong with Gabriel?" I asked as we surveyed this unusual scene.

When we finally got to him, he told us that he had hooked the biggest Northern Pike he had ever seen only for it to get away just as he got it to shore. Along with the fish went his favorite lure. Apparently, after the line broke the huge fish spit out his lure which was tied a few feet below a floating bobber.

To rescue his lure, he climbed into his canoe—a two-person model with only him in it.

On his way back from a successful lure recovery, a huge gust of wind from an incoming storm picked up the front of the canoe and flipped it over.

While his canoe—the one his dad was going to have to pay for—was sinking about 100 feet offshore, our oldest son Gehrig dove in to help while I sat down and took off my hiking boots before joining in the canoe recovery. Sarah thought it seemed somewhat odd to bother with my boots until that evening when I explained the physics of water-filled boots on the ability to swim effectively.

We managed to get the canoe back to land where the lovely Minnesota summer turned to late Fall in a matter of seconds.

Dripping wet—and missing his best knife that fell into the bottom of the lake—Gabriel helped transport his canoe through the woods until our shivering made seeking warmth a very appealing endeavor.

There is a great deal of satisfaction from finding enough buried pine straw and twigs to get a fire started in a rainstorm. It is even better when you get the fire to a place where even wet wood will burn and keep you warm enough to ride out a storm. The key is to keep piling on the wood so that even in torrential rains you will still have some flame to help restart it in between storms.

But patience is the key in the great North Woods and in the Maritimes because, as Yogi Berra once said, "It ain't over till it's over."

The experts are divided somewhat on how safe it is to use a Kevlar canoe for a temporary shelter. Sitting on a personal flotation device, away from large trees and away from open spaces is recommended, but nature is still going to do what it wants to do.

The experts are not divided on what to do if your hair begins to stand on end during an approaching storm.

In 2024 I was hiking with Sarah and Gabriel on the Scarp Ridge trail near Crested Butte, Colorado. This trail is famous for views that make people think of Switzerland. It is also a trail that peaks at 11,867 feet where you are the tallest thing around.

We were admiring the majestic views after a very arduous climb. The clouds had been gathering throughout our hike, but so far we had not seen any lightning or heard any distant thunder. It seemed that this weather system would pass over us without incident when Gabriel looked at his mother and announced, "Mom, your hair is standing on end."

It sure was.

She has very curly, long hair that was indeed much less curly and reaching for the sky.

She then looked up at me, and asked, "Am I about to be struck by lightning?!?" I was sure the flapping arms were eminent.

If you can keep the person you are hiking with from pressing the panic button of all panic buttons you can calmly tell them to drop to their knees and bend forward because, according to the National Weather Service, they are indeed about to be struck by lightning.

One problem. That day I was not aware of this recommendation. I did know that running would dramatically increase the odds of being struck. I also knew that if I overreacted or told her to get down and bend forward, she would have taken off in a full sprint—especially since she also claimed to have a tingling feeling in her foot.

Being ignorant that day the best I could muster was to look at Gabriel and mouth, "Let's go." I calmly told Sarah to take Jake and start heading for lower ground right away. She and Jake did just that on what looked, at times, like it was about to be a track meet.

When we got to the bottom of the trail, she claimed that the tingling in her foot was probably from a "little lighting strike."

I did not disagree with her . . .

4

Suffering without Silence

One of the requirements of being an effective tent camper is to learn how to value the application of intestinal fortitude to dozens, if not hundreds, of inconveniences.

This does not mean, however, that you should not feel free to complain about it.

In fact, this chapter is devoted to the long list of things that you should gripe about. It will make the great parts of camping (Chapter Five) become even greater and will aid in creating amnesia while you are back in civilization. This amnesia is critical in mustering up excitement for your next camping trip.

What follows is a list—in no particular order of importance or applicability—of the fleeting misery you must be able to deal with in order to have a great time when you are not miserable.

Sharing the Planet with Humans

My wife once said, "Hotel people should go to hotels and camping people should go camping."

That simple sentiment holds up very well when you find yourself tent camping in the United States and even parts of Canada that are close enough to the US for those Canadians to learn how we act in public.

Part of the problem, I think, is that a lot of people believe that staying at the KOA is real camping. Others believe that being in a huge RV with the news blaring from a television set is real camping. Still other people think that the new trend of so-called "glamping" is camping.

Therefore, when people leave the cities for a weekend of "camping" they tend to bring the city with them no matter where they settle.

On the rare occasions where my wife and I have ended up in one of these nightmarish collections of humanity, we find ourselves wondering how one species can be so obnoxious.

Why, for example, do people need a television or music while venturing out into nature? I would argue that the goal should be to not even remember who the President of the United States is after a few days living under the stars. TikTok, Instagram, Facebook, and all the other social media platforms should not even work in the woods. Neither should generators, butane lighters, space heaters, or fake firewood that is covered in plastic.

Of course, as any serious tent camper knows, much of this can be avoided by simply finding primitive, out of the way camping sites far from humanity.

If you camp in the backcountry this will not be an issue unless you take idiots along with you.

If you camp in more primitive traditional sites, it is less likely to occur.

If you camp anywhere else, the morons will likely find you.

When you first start tent camping you will see signs on many campgrounds that mention something about "Quiet Hours." These signs clearly say that after 10 p.m., or so, all campers need to keep the noise down so others can rest.

You can take the Quiet Hours sign and use it to start your first fire because all over the United States you will find that no one cares that you are trying to sleep, or that your children are not used to hearing major profanity being used by preschoolers and their grandparents in the adjoining campsite.

You will find that here in the States, people take their loud cell phone conversations, their domestic squabbles, and their proclivity for drinking twelve gallons of beer in one sitting and bring all of it camping.

Heck, if you are lucky, you will even get to hear blaring rap or country music from the vehicles parked nearby.

But Americans do not have a monopoly on camping ignorance.

Somewhere in Quebec resides a young woman who has a severe sinus and attitude issue.

We discovered this when she pulled up next to us in the Chignecto campground in Fundy National Park at about midnight. With her car running and headlights illuminating her tent pad, our tent site, and much of the rest of our loop, she proceeded to loudly—and repeatedly—snort like John Candy in *Planes, Trains and Automobiles* to clear her sinuses. When she was not clearing her nasal passages or banging her gear, she would take time to yell at her dog in French. I did not have access to Google translate but I think she was saying, "*Tais-toi pour que je puisse m'entendre renifler*" which translates to "Be quiet so I can hear myself snort."

About two hours later she finally fell asleep—and began snoring. Loudly.

I share this not to discourage anyone from joining the millions of Americans who go tent camping every year. I say this so that anyone new to camping can try to find facilities that create the fewest human interactions possible.

It is just unavoidable sometimes.

Sharing the Bathroom with Other Disgusting Humans

Of all the things I miss about being home, my bathroom quickly emerges at the top of the list.

Sometimes I find myself camping in an area with decent showers, cleanish toilets, and running water in a sink.

Often, all I find is a pit toilet (this is a hole dug into the ground out in the woods where flies come up under you to say hello), an outhouse, or a bathroom that has not been serviced since Jimmy Carter was president.

Compounding matters is the sharing of these facilities with other bipeds that carry their own smells and make unique noises.

It helps, for those people camping with a partner, if both people gripe about these conditions. It is not helpful if one partner misses this part of civilization, and the other does not.

Since 2020 Sarah and I have spent most of our camping nights in Colorado where our youngest son works on a ranch and as a whitewater rafting guide.

The campground we use has a small outhouse that is serviced every February 29, but not much more than that.

I dread my first trip into this nasty little house. The fly population is close to that of China and the toilet paper is so thin and rough that you would prefer a high-grit sandpaper.

Yet, every year her first words to me are, "Boy, get in there with your fly friends."

This is just cruel. But she is significantly tougher than I am when we camp so I say, "Yes, ma'am" and skulk away. But not before I grab my own roll of Charmin and tell her that I will not live like an animal.

Things do not get much better when we find campgrounds with more "luxurious" accommodations.

At Cape Lookout State Park, along the coast of Oregon, we came upon a shower that was somehow able to shoot out icicles instead of warm water.

These piercing, needle-like blasts of water had me screaming so loud that Sarah could not hear herself laughing in the women's shower next door.

In Newfoundland's Gros Morne National Park, we had showers that you had to keep pressing a button on the wall to activate. The only problem was that after you pressed the button you got what seemed to be about 10 seconds of water.

I may have to have an elbow replacement from that experience alone. Then, upon getting out of this shower you step into an area that is about the size of a phone booth (for those who remember these) to dry off.

The floor is covered with mud from the humans who came before you. So, one of the tricks you learn as a camper is how to put one piece of your own dirty clothing on this mud, step out like a ballerina and dry yourself enough to begin the process of putting on damp, clean clothes that will have some mud on them by the time you exit. My wife reminded me that, while this is my method, some people have slightly more refined processes for this endeavor like wearing shower shoes or stepping onto a pair of sandals. But one thing everyone will agree on is that navigating dressing in a mud puddle is not easy and certainly a reason to gripe.

Speaking of mud, in the New Discovery State Park in Vermont, I sloshed through the mud that the remnants of Hurricane Lee left behind, for what seemed like half a mile to the shower facilities only to find my own "new discovery" that the shower was coin operated. You read that right. **COIN** operated. The box and dial that was attached to it dated to somewhere around the signing of the Declaration of Independence. And, of course, as I fed it quarters and put the dial on "HOT," the only thing that came out were drizzles of very un-hot water.

So, after banging on this metal box for twenty minutes and cursing with each justifiable blow, I put my dirty clothes back on and trudged to the campground entrance to inquire about finding a shower that was built after 1980.

I was directed to the shower that was ADA accessible. It had two shower heads—one high, one low. The low one was about 2.5 feet above the ground. Guess which one did not work?

Yep, the high one.

I am not a tall person but crouching down on the ground in a semi-fetal position to take a shower was not exactly what I preferred.

But at least I was alone.

Sharing campground bathrooms with strangers always makes me wonder, "Would I ever invite the person next to me to come into my bathroom at home and do what they are doing while I am doing this at the same time?"

No, I would not. But there you sit as a person only inches from you, and separated only by a thin, fake-wood wall, carries on with their own intestinal orchestra.

Bathing When There Is No Shower

Genuinely embracing being outdoors often means many days spent hiking into the wilderness. It can also mean mountain biking, rock climbing, wood gathering, and many more activities that make you sweat.

There are very few things more awful than getting out of the clothes you were sweating in and climbing into your sleeping bag with a layer of grime coating your body.

The ability to overcome this situation depends on many factors. One of them is your tolerance for ice cold water in the absence of a normal shower.

From an early age my sons learned what it was like to climb into a frigid river with a sponge and some ultra eco-friendly soap to bathe.

In fact, one of their favorite stories that they were all too happy to share with friends was how I made them go into a river in Canada's Glacier National Park when there was still more than a foot of ice and snow on both banks.

Teenagers at the time, I thought it might be the first time one of them would suggest a fist fight rather than following my instructions. But these boys were well past ripe and there is nothing more awful smelling than a ripe teenage boy. So, they finally complied—head to toe—and years later when one of their Florida friends would complain about something they would chime in with, "Man, that is nothing. We used to take a bath in frozen rivers in Canada with snow on the banks!"

It brought a proud tear to my eye to hear their recounting of this story.

The key to bathing in water that is between 32.1 and 32.9 degrees is to go into it with the wonderful payoff in mind—and go into the water about one inch at a time.

Washing your back—male or female—will be nearly the worst of it. Depending on your gender, other areas will be more shocking to submerge.

Interestingly, the longer you are in there, the better it feels—mostly because in my experience this is when the numbness sets in, while nearing the earliest and safest stages of hypothermia. (Note: I am not a doctor, or even an expert on hypothermia and therefore cannot recommend this kind of behavior. Some experts do recommend it under certain circumstances for health benefits; however, I cannot speak to that either. I only know that this is the best way I know to survive camping without a shower.)

If you should choose to indulge in this activity I have a couple quick tips to offer.

Have soft, cozy clothes and a good towel handy on a rock nearby.

One more item . . .

It is best to do this when it is dark lest you provide free entertainment for anyone who might be admiring the river. And keep your head on a swivel in case curious random animals stop by to inspect your cleaning techniques (as Sarah discovered when a muskrat came up on a rock two feet away and stared at her while she was washing her face).

We have noticed that once we stop shaking and regain the feeling in our toes, we sleep like a baby.

That is, until we wake up in the middle of a cold night and need to go to the outhouse…

I do not have any medical evidence to prove this, but I am certain cold air makes your bladder contract.

The problem is that when you are a tent camper in areas or times of the year when it is cold, you usually wear warm socks, base layer thermals and maybe sweatpants, a thermal top, hooded sweatshirt (hood over your head), and maybe even gloves. Then you climb into a mummy sleeping bag and perhaps have the old-fashioned sleeping bag over you as a comforter.

When your bladder wakes you up in the middle of the night you can first try lying on your side to buy twenty minutes or so. But there comes a point where you realize that you either get up and go outside or you do something that you have not done since you were a year and a half old.

Getting out of a mummy bag is not unlike pretending to be Harry Houdini breaking out of chains. If you are sharing a tent with other living beings, they will most assuredly wake up as you kick and fight and curse.

Then, you must find the tent zipper—that is if your partner has not dog-proofed it like mine did one year.

Our brilliant dog had figured out how to use his nose to nudge the zipper up on our tent. This is the same dog that used his little teeth to open a tent by grabbing the zipper and running with it, on only the second night he had ever gone camping.

So, without telling me, my wife used some sort of vintage paper clip to fasten the tent zipper and keep Jake from making a break for it.

Without my contact lenses, I have 20/400 vision in both eyes.

When you are legally blind and need to get to the fly-ridden outhouse quickly, the last thing you need is some paper clip engineered to be a dog lock. This leads to more cursing, broken paper clips, and sprinting to the closest tree rather than the more civilized facilities.

Sleeping with Other Humans When You Cannot Bathe

I think I came close to taking complete leave of my senses in the summer of 2013.

Having dragged our flooded tent to the Cape Breton dumpster earlier in our vacation—and being somewhat reluctant to pay retail for a new one—we arrived at Baxter State Park in Maine to begin an eight-day backcountry trip into the land of Stephen King, black flies, and gorgeous scenery.

The trek involved the usual canvas refrigerators on our backs—minus the King James Bible—and lasted for mile after grueling mile.

One highlight, I suppose, was fording a river with all our gear. That is until I managed to step into a low spot in Maine's answer to the Nile. Instantly, my pack went from 45 pounds to about 145 pounds.

Enjoying a shallow part of our Maine river crossing. At least no piranhas appeared.

That night we arrived exhausted and sweaty.

It was at this precise moment as we began to set up camp when Gehrig and Gabriel realized that their father—a man who buys all his clothes at garage sales and thrift stores and picks up pennies on the ground—had not bothered to buy another tent.

They also learned that when you see a tent advertised as "four-person" that means four people lying 1 millimeter apart from one another. It does not mean four people lying there comfortably with a little elbow room.

That first night I learned something amazing about our son, Gabriel.

Incredibly, when he snores, he sounds exactly like Curly from the old *Three Stooges* program.

"Zzzznggghhhhwoowoowoowoo" is approximately what this sounds like.

It would have been hilarious to his brother and my wife had I not been near him snoring like an asthmatic brontosaurus.

The next day—and during daylight hours the rest of our time near Mount Katahdin—we had a wonderful vacation even though the state bird of Maine should be the black fly. Every morning we would spray high-DEET repellent—also known as poison—on our clothes before we ventured out.

Day after day we hiked, canoed, fished for Brook trout, ate wild berries, and then enjoyed the fire each night until we all realized that as we grew tired, the inevitable unzipping of the small tent was going to take place.

One night as delirium was beginning to set in, I looked at Sarah and pathetically declared, "I am a DEET-covered dirt ball."

I then crawled into the tent and resumed snoring.

Sharing Is Caring—and Annoying

If you are new to tent camping there is an important unwritten rule that you need to know about. It is called "Campers Rules," and it basically tells you that you should always be prepared to spread the wealth with other campers. This applies to people in your campsite as well as strangers nearby.

The idea is that camping trips are often accompanied by forgetfulness or unexpected circumstances. Maybe you will forget bug spray or a spatula.

Perhaps your matches (never bring a city-slicker lighter camping . . .) are not dry enough. Maybe you need some salt for your dinner. Whatever.

In a wonderful example of what some might call voluntary socialism, tent campers tend to be extremely generous. Even though I am a devout capitalist I even derive a great deal of pleasure from giving a fellow camper firewood or matches or some food.

The inherent problem with sharing is that sometimes the people you share with are somewhat unaware of the concept of scarce resources and self-preservation.

I have camped with people who did not bring enough food, stand over my shoulder watching me as I ate dinner, waiting for me to split my steak—STEAK!!—in half.

I have also experienced folks sitting at camp with NO FOOD because they thought somehow the camping invitation came with an all-you-can eat free buffet. When handed a bottle of a kind of pricey maple syrup to go with their free pancakes, one guy—who shall remain nameless—poured about a third of the entire bottle over his breakfast.

And then there is camping with home-schooling families with an average of nine and a half kids each.

One winter many, many years ago I had the brilliant idea of organizing a camping trip to the Ichetucknee State Park in Florida. This park is famous for crystal clear spring water, manatees, and world-class canoeing through the jungles of north Central Florida.

Conservatively, I estimate that fifty people—maybe more depending on babies born during that trip—showed up to set up tents and enjoy what little nature Florida has left.

For our trip to Ichetucknee I let everyone know that I would make a giant pot of beef and venison chili, which is a perfect tent camping meal.

Later in this book I will provide my recipe for chili. This will be the only recipe in the book but will be worth every penny to you if you follow it. That is because in addition to being the greatest dishwasher in the world, I also may very well make the greatest bowl of chili in the *history of the world*.

Since the ingredients I use are expensive and the quantity I was making would feed a small army, I politely asked each family to kick in a few bucks to help defray my costs.

The next morning, I woke up with about $1.77 in my pocket, which was the same amount of money I had when we arrived.

No problem, I thought. At least everyone will have enough money to enjoy our canoe trip today.

Right.

Upon realizing that the local outfitters, you know, *charged money* to rent canoes, every family, except for maybe one, packed up and went home.

In fairness to them, when you have between six and sixteen kids there may not be much disposable income left over to shell out for chili or canoeing.

But that means that if you are going camping with other people, make sure they have no kids or are rich.

Or go by yourself and share with strangers who you will never see again and think, "You know, you still owe me for chili. . . ."

Camping with the Government

As I am writing this chapter, I have been a professional economist for thirty-six years. I have been a Libertarian since the day I was born. The combination of these two realities makes it very difficult to deal with one of the greatest fun-killers known to human beings.

Government.

Thomas Paine once wrote, "Government, even in its best state, is but a necessary evil; in its worst state, an intolerable one." Mr. Paine must have written *Common Sense* while on a tent camping trip.

When you go camping in the States you will discover some strangely absurd rules and regulations along with blatant economic stupidity on lands managed by our government.

First, there is the fourteen-day rule.

All over the United States you will come across campgrounds run by the federal or state government that tell you that you can only camp in a certain place for fourteen days in a thirty-day period, or more than thirty days in a year. After fourteen days, you must move at least three miles away and can't camp in the same national forest or grassland for more than twenty-eight days in a sixty-day period.

One example we deal with every summer is at Granite Campground near Almont, Colorado. This primitive campground (one fly-filled outhouse) has only six sites along the beautiful Taylor River. Every site is a walk-in, first-come, first-served location.

Because of the primitive nature of this location, you will rarely see more than one or two sites with anyone on them. For five years we watched this reality unfold. Most nights, night after night, we are the only campers around.

If you ran a motel with six rooms and virtually every night only one family was in your motel, what would you do when that family had reached fourteen nights?

Would you kick them out and now earn zero dollars per night, or would you gladly take their money if they were clean, quiet, peaceful, and willing to pay up?

If you ran this motel and noticed that your current pricing structure was leading to less demand than supply, would you keep your prices stable, or lower them?

Well, the United States government does not operate under the same rational, market-based principles of a motel.

On more than one occasion I have tried to stay more than fourteen days. I pay the nightly fee, keep our campground quiet and clean, and even dispose of trash around other campsites that the government has failed to maintain.

Inevitably, one or more Forest Service employees come out to our site and begin explaining why we need to leave, including one day when it was raining, and I was trying to take a nap. Instead, I stood there in the rain giving an impromptu lecture on how to run a business.

No matter what form of logic, reason, or free economics lessons I provide for them, they just keep saying, "Rules are rules."

That is a stupid answer.

When I ask, "Why is it a rule? Who made this a rule? Does this rule make any sense?" They stare at me as if I am an alien who has just landed on the land of rules.

Compounding matters is the inefficient business practices the government uses.

One year online it showed that campsites at this location were $12 but when we got to the campground and saw the bulletin board it had one sign showing a price of $18 and another sign showing $16. What if a local restaurant did that? How long would they be in business?

Making matters worse, government officials do not even address the unsold sites and ask, "Gee, should we lower prices to get more customers?"

And they miss what hotels routinely do—charge more for the better spots.

The location we always pick is by far the nicest site at this campground. It costs the same as the ones in full sun and right by the parking lot.

I have tried to explain to government officials that they should try variable rate pricing based on the popularity of the camping sites; lower prices when demand is not meeting supply and drop the fourteen-day rule (supposedly designed to keep people from being squatters) and allow people who can prove they are not vagrants to pay a premium for stays that last longer.

This free economics seminar is always ignored so we pack up and move several miles away.

Then there is the firewood issue . . .

You may have noticed that over the past several years forest fires keep raging all over the western United States and parts of Canada.

But when is the last time your heard about forests managed by Georgia Pacific or Weyerhaeuser burning to the ground?

You haven't.

The reason is simple. Private, for-profit timber companies have the proper motivation and face the full consequences of their behavior.

If a timber company fails to manage its lands effectively and a lightning strike burns its forests to the ground, it will lose all the profit it could have earned from those trees.

The motivation of the company is profit. The consequences of lax management are losses and possible bankruptcy.

On the other hand, if you go into forests managed by state and federal governments you will see dead trees and brush all over the ground as far as you can walk. These trees are the perfect fuel to create the sort of devastating fires we have seen over the years.

But what is the motivation of the government to do anything about it? It is not-for-profit and is guaranteed to get our tax dollars to keep its doors open.

So even if federal officials blow it and half of California burns to the ground there are no measurable consequences. The Forest Service can look all of us in the face and ask, "So what are you going to do about our malfeasance? Nothing." We cannot deduct from our taxes the money we feel has been wasted on the ineptitude of government officials.

Which brings me to required permits to gather firewood all over the country.

Clearly, no one who cares about nature wants to see some idiot cutting down trees to get wood for cooking hot dogs.

But, what about gathering dead wood off the ground? In state after state, you will see federal requirements that you get a permit to gather downed wood. Some of the offices you would have to drive to in order to get a permit can be hours from your campsite.

Thus, without the permit you become a criminal if you help clear the forest floor of the fuel that helps forests burn.

Meanwhile, near your camp host there will likely be an area where you can pay the government near-monopoly prices for a bundle of firewood.

The Canadian government is not immune from the disease of economic illiteracy either.

From British Columbia to New Brunswick, you will routinely encounter a strange policy that applies to building a campfire.

Unlike in the US where you pay for the wood you burn—causing rationing and careful fire considerations—in many national parks in Canada you pay to buy a firewood burning permit and then the park supplies you with wood. All the wood you want.

The thinking, according to well-meaning Canadian officials I have talked to, is that by charging people to have a fire it would reduce total permit purchases, lead to fewer fires and less climate-damaging smoke from the forest guests.

Instead, what I have witnessed (even at our site) is that once you have your burn permit you feel like you need to get your money's worth and thus it is not uncommon to see campfires that look more like what Tom Hanks lit in *Castaway* to signal passing ships. Translation? You will see bonfires all over the national parks of Canada.

Dish Washing with No Sink in Sight

I take great pride in my willingness and ability to properly wash dishes. I am so good at it, in fact, that my youngest son once said to his mother (when he was about five), "Mom, you are the prettiest." He then looked at me and said, "And Dad is the dishest."

There it is.

Having skills limited to gathering firewood, cooking, and doing dishes, I have had to figure out the most efficient way to carry out this task in dozens of camping situations.

If you ever camp somewhere that has a large utility sink there will often be a sign next to it telling you not to do dishes in the sink.

So, most of the time I find myself taking a large, collapsible bucket down to a river or stream where I fill it with water, tote it back to our campsite and use either a large rock or our portable cooking grate to wash dishes on.

I always miss my dishwasher almost as much as my private toilet within seconds.

The water is freezing cold. It sloshes around and flies on me while I wash dishes. When we cook something with butter or grease or oil, I stand there and scrub for what seems like hours. And, since rocks are not always flat, I often find myself retrieving dishes that are attempting to slide away.

Then, I take the bucket back to the river, fill it with clean water, walk back to camp and rinse each item.

Paper plates and plastic cups and utensils can fix a lot of this unless you are either trying to reduce the trash you create or are in parts of eastern Canada where you cannot even buy plastic utensils.

Air Mattress Dos and Don'ts

Thankfully, you can still buy air mattresses made of plastic.

But if you choose to buy an air mattress for your tent prepare to fill it with air about once a week. If you do not do this, you and your partner will feel like you are ground beef inside a hard-shell taco. It is also a fact that if you are lying on a partially deflated air mattress when your partner plops down on it you will fly about 3 feet in the air.

One more thing. NEVER attempt to stand on any mattress to do yoga while your partner is sleeping. It might lead to a heart attack . . .

One night on a faraway lake in Minnesota with no ambulances nearby, Sarah decided to stand on one foot and do some stretching exercises she had seen in some stupid yoga video. I woke up just as she lost her balance and was screaming while falling on top of me. In my dazed state she appeared to be thirteen feet tall with wild hair. My chest pains lasted the rest of the night, and I told her, more than once, that if I did not make it and she ever remarried, I would come back as a squirrel, run right up her pants leg, and bite her.

That is when she revealed that she had snuck an emergency flip phone into her pack "just in case." That turned my heart attack into an "are you kidding me?" mini seizure.

Being kind of a hippie, her reaction to my heart and seizure issues was to reach into her large bag of vitamins and supplements and start pulling out fish oil and other stuff she thought might help. A prescription for morphine would have been better.

But then again, given my experience with my own prescriptions, the fish oil and Ashwagandha might have been smarter options.

Doing Stupid Things

In 2020 I suffered a ruptured bicep tendon playing pickleball, of all things, and was given some pain meds before we left for a long canoe camping trip.

I was hurting after portaging my canoe out of the Boundary Waters, so that night I thought a half a pain pill would help.

I woke up with a bright red rash, burning skin, and shortness of breath.

Trying not to send my wife into another arm-flapping panic, I quietly woke up Gabriel and asked him to look up poisonous plants of northern Minnesota.

That is because surely, I could not have been stupid enough to take a half a pain pill on a mostly empty stomach. Surely . . .

Gabriel ended up speeding me to the Ely, Minnesota, emergency room while I kept wheezing and telling him to slow down at the red lights.

A huge I.V. of Benadryl later I was feeling somewhat loopy, fantastic and, once again, kind of dumb.

For me, being kind of dumb while on vacation stems, in part, from being frugal on vacation. In 2023 I took two pairs of hiking boots with me out west. One was kind of old, the other pair was brand new. I was going to save the brand-new ones for when we got to Canada in the fall.

Sarah noticed that I was slipping on some of our hikes when I should have been more sure-footed. She also pointed out how the soles were beginning to separate from the boot. Yet, instead of breaking out the new boots early I asked her to text our neighbor in Florida and ask her to go in my closet, find my other old hiking boots, and mail them to me.

The way I figured it I could repair the ones that were giving me trouble, use the even older ones being mailed to me as backup, and THEN save the new ones for Canada.

So that is what I did. The shoe glue and clamps worked great, and I saved my new boots for, well, 2024. I just couldn't bring myself to hit the trails wearing perfectly good boots when I had two well-worn, repaired, and broken-in old ones.

Just like I could not let myself drive to a health clinic when I ran a large, trebled fishhook entirely through my thumb after trying to free a fish in the Kawishiwi River. After driving several miles with one good hand I stopped at

How an economist saves money on boots

the same bait shop where I had bought the hook and in front of some squeamish customers had the owner of the shop cut off the end of the hook and run the shaft back out of my thumb. A couple of dollars' worth of disinfectant supplies later, and I was back in business.

I am grateful that I saved money on medical bills because I needed some extra cash when I told Sarah our cooler and cargo carrier would be fine on the back of our car since we were in Minnesota—the land of nice people. That evening a less than nice person stole our cargo carrier but only after an equally not-nice bear destroyed the cooler.

But at least I have never been stupid enough to voluntarily camp where it is hot at night.

One of the smartest things I ever imparted on my sons was to tell them, "Boys, never—and I mean never—go tent camping anywhere the temperature might be above 68 degrees at night."

Nevertheless, their destination for, "I forgot what Dad said," was the Everglades—in the summer. The middle of summer.

After spending a nice day with their friend in the Florida Keys they drove for hours to a campsite that was shockingly empty to set up a three-person tent (remember, this means one millimeter of space between each person).

When Gabriel entered, he discovered his brother and buddy lying there, sweating and gasping for any humid air they could find.

The temperature outside, at midnight, was a balmy 99 degrees. Inside the tent it was closer to the core of the Earth. So, they chose to leave.

Much later the next morning, the three finally made it to the park's visitor center where they went upstairs to try to sneak in a little sleep. What they did not count on was the reaction of park guests who also wanted to go upstairs but did not expect to find teenagers in sleeping bags on the floor.

5

The Best Parts of Tent Camping

Now that we have covered all the reasons to stay home or book a nice, climate-controlled resort for your next vacation, we turn our attention to what you may be missing by not shucking all aspects of civilization in favor of unzipping your small bedroom each night.

There is a reason why millions of people choose to brave the wilds in PU coated polyester every year. There are things about tent camping that are so glorious that enduring bears, drunks, earthquakes (our trip to Idaho in 1999), and dirt are all more than worth it.

Here is what non-campers are missing . . .

Real Sleep

One of the more serious health concerns—especially since the invention of the awful cell phone—is the lack of sleep, especially for teenagers, that we are getting in the United States.

If you leave your phone by a rock and/or have no cell phone service while camping, you will be almost instantly rewarded with, and amazed by, your body's ability to recognize that the sun has gone down and then come back up.

It will not be uncommon to feel your eyes grow heavy long before they would if you were in the light-polluted urban areas of the US. Eight to ten hours later, your eyes will open to the likely sound of melodic birds nearby and you will feel years younger (assuming you keep your mattress properly aired).

Sarah—ever the nutrition and health advisor—told me that studies have found that even a weekend of camping (absent of cell phone blue light interference in the evening) can shift circadian rhythms and help reset our body clocks. I don't know what circadian means, but she is right.

This glorious part of camping is so incredibly regenerative that, when people ask us what the highlight of our summer was, we often say, "Sleeping."

But sometimes we ignore our better judgment and choose not to rough it.

Since I never get away with anything, the two times Sarah and I consciously decided to forgo tent camping for more urban accommodations we learned in a hurry why tents, with all their issues, are better if you care about sleeping with both eyes closed.

The first time was in 2003 when we were in New York. Rather than pitch camp along the Hudson River and take a day trip into New York City, we decided to travel to the city by train and then travel back to our more civilized lodging in Irvington that night.

Big mistake.

Shortly after 4 p.m. I was walking out of Central Park with the kids in tow when I noticed what seemed like the entire planet milling around on the sidewalks as far as the eye could see. Minutes later Sarah met up with us and at that moment we learned that a blackout had hit the city.

Gehrig had found a big stick in Central Park that he was carrying around which I thought we might have to use later that evening.

With no train service—and therefore no way out of Manhattan—we started walking in the direction of an apartment building where one of Sarah's high-school friends lived.

One slight problem came up during our several hours of walking. A couple of days earlier, the stroller we were using to transport Gabriel had lost a wheel and his penny-pinching father had not yet replaced it. Some polite New Yorkers saw our poor son in a his three-wheeled stroller and made extra room for us as we pitifully ventured down the sidewalks.

Not far into our long walk we looked up and saw Rudy Giuliani walking toward us in the crowd. I took this as a good omen since we were just a couple of years removed from 9/11 and I felt that he managed that day well.

When we finally made it to her friend's apartment, we found that New York City has a lot of stairs when the elevators are not working.

A few hours after our arrival as we were settling in for a safe, relaxing evening, her old friend entered the living room and asked the worst question possible.

"So, where are you guys staying this evening?"

I do not remember what we said at that moment because years later the shock of that question has not worn off.

But I do remember that we left to see what hotels were open in the area as the sun was beginning to make its way down over a city that in the past did not fare too well (1977 came to mind) when all the lights went out.

With every hotel clerk laughing in our face as we got halfway through the question, "Do you have any rooms available?" we walked back to her building, back up the stairs and knocked on her door.

At that moment, as carefully, kindly, and firmly as I could possibly say it, I informed Sarah's friend that we were staying with her. Period.

I missed being in a tent in the woods that night as the sun went down, and the many police and ambulance sirens began wailing—and kept on wailing.

The next morning, we headed to Grand Central Station in the hopes that we could catch our train back up the Hudson.

It was like a movie scene where every time the announcer called out any train on any track desperate human beings bolted for freedom.

When he finally said our train over the loudspeaker, I took that three-wheeled stroller and ran like Barry Sanders (look him up on YouTube) through swarms of people with the rest of my family sprinting and weaving behind me.

When we got on the train, and it started moving I thought we had won the lottery. Then the power went out . . . again. This time, it was only momentary and in short order we were rolling out of the city and past several "urban campers" that had their tents set up in places where blackouts did not matter as much.

The second time I wished we were in a tent instead of a place with a real roof came in 2017 when we traveled to Cape Breton for the Celtic Colours International Festival that is held in October every year.

This time, we picked an Airbnb in Mabou, Nova Scotia.

I would have preferred the Chumley House.

It was a dark, rainy night when we met up with the man we were renting the house from. We followed him way out in the country to a remote home that, according to the photos, was very charming and had a wonderful view of the Fall colors in that region.

It also had no locking doors, two boxes of the board game, "How to Host a Murder" (why two?) and a vacuum cleaner that the host told us to use at night to get rid of the swarms of house flies that tended to come into the bedroom even though there were no doors or windows left open.

Sarah never saw *The Amityville Horror,* so the fly thing was weird, but not terrifying to her.

I had one eye open the entire time we were there. Sarah, quite fittingly, managed to find a huge axe that she kept in our bedroom while we braced the door with a large old chair.

I do not recall ever doing any of these things while tent camping.

Five-Minute Friends

As we were preparing for a hike in Canada's Jasper National Park (put this place on your bucket list), Sarah spotted a sign telling hikers that we were about to enter wolverine territory. The wolverine is my favorite animal and having never seen one in the wild I was beyond excited.

"Look at what the sign says, Jack. It says that wolverines are antisocial and cantankerous—just like you!"

I think that was a compliment, but I did not seek clarification.

Because I am a little bit like a wolverine, over the course of my life, I have discovered that often the best kind of friends are what my family calls, "five-minute friends." I specialize in making friends in that category.

When I meet someone while camping—whether it is a neighbor or someone I might encounter out on a trail, I do not have enough time to find out what all their faults are, so it is easier to get a good impression (that is unless they do not talk to you at Mt. St. Helens . . .)

These friends have included Canadians who taught us how to play cricket, numerous camp hosts who are some of the most interesting and nicest retirees on the planet (including the man whose job in the 1960s was to guard Lee Harvey Oswald's gravesite), many young people who have restored our hope for the future, and adults who have provided us with shelter, recovered lost property, and given us enjoyable political conversations or free leeches.

Yes, leeches.

The first time we ever ventured into Minnesota (2005) we camped in Bears Head State Park near Ely (one of the best small towns in America).

We were preparing for a day of fishing when we met a guy who told us not to bother going to the bait shop because he had just what we needed.

When he opened a small Styrofoam bucket to reveal the bait of choice for this part of the world all I could think of was the scene from the movie *Stand by Me* when the kids came out of a small pond covered with blood-sucking leeches all over them. I did not want to seem ungrateful, but I kept wondering how you get a leech on a hook when it is stuck to your hand, face, or other parts of your body.

Perhaps sensing my skepticism, this polite Minnesotan showed us how to get them out and on the hook without having our blood drained first, and from then on we have always used this unusual bait.

In 2023 Sarah and I met a young French-Canadian who might be Prime Minister of that country someday.

We had just finished dinner when this lovely ten-year-old pulled up to our camp on her bicycle. In broken English she explained to us that she had made some bracelets that she was selling to raise money for materials she needed to build her rabbits a little house.

Her pitch was not whiny, nor did she seem entitled. She showed us her selection, explained her pricing model, and smiled.

We bought a couple of her lovely bracelets, paying her in the stronger US dollar (explaining exchange rates along the way), and then we both watched as this little entrepreneur rode all over the campground marketing her product. She was out so late that her mother had to go find her. When she finally did, this youngster had a stack of cash that would have made Elon Musk blush.

In 2014 we were traveling through South Dakota when suddenly a combination of tornadic activity combined with hail the size of baseballs and sheets of torrential rain descended upon us.

We tried to pull our car under some trees near the side of a road that was in the middle of nowhere, but it was not helping.

Out of nowhere a pickup truck came by and the driver waved at us to follow him.

He could have been a wanted criminal, and I would have stayed right on his bumper.

He pulled into this huge airport hangar-looking building and directed us inside.

As the hail and wind pounded this building, we shared the standard greetings mixed with profuse thanks for his kindness.

At one point during the conversation, he mentioned that he had visited Florida once while in a rodeo.

"So, do they make it worth your while so you can cover your costs?" asked Mrs. Chambless.

He paused, looked a little funny, smiled politely, and said, "I do OK."

Had my wife known who our newest five-minute friend was she would have crawled into the nearest gopher hole on the South Dakota plains.

About a month later she and the boys were at the Calgary Stampede—the Super Bowl of rodeos—when the saddle bronc competition was about to begin.

"And now, please welcome two-time World Champion, Chad Ferley"!

Ironically, Chad Ferley was the name of the guy we hung out with in South Dakota and his picture at the Calgary Stampede matched the person named Chad Ferley that day in his hanger.

For some reason, my wife slumped down in her seat as if someone was about to point at her and say, "Hey aren't you the girl who asked Chad Ferley if he made enough money to cover his costs?!??"

Speaking of cash, allow me to offer up some tips for not losing yours—and how five-minute friends are invaluable when you do.

For some odd reason, when I leave home for any camping trip the first thing I start doing is misplacing my wallet and keys. As I get older, my poor wife has taken to looking at me as if I am only weeks away from forgetting her name.

Most of the time my wallet and/or keys show up somewhere in the auxiliary tent I keep close by as my personal closet. Being on vacation this closet looks like a pig's stie most of the time, hence the trouble finding things.

But the real trouble begins when I leave my wallet on top of the car while getting gasoline. . . .

In 1998 I pulled this stunt in Seattle on the day we were supposed to drive to British Columbia, where something like a driver's license comes in handy.

When I got to the Canadian border it dawned on me that somewhere miles behind me were my identification, my cash, credit cards, and a coupon for a free car wash the next time we were in Louisiana.

Knowing that the Canadian government was not going to take my word for it, I made the long U-turn and began the "this trip is probably over" drive back to Seattle.

I traced our "steps" back to the last gas station we had stopped at. Then, in a moment of complete and utter naivete, I called the nearest police office to report a lost wallet.

Unbeknownst to me, there are five-minute friends whom we never meet while we are trying to make it from campsite to campsite.

The police told me that a lady named Desiree had found my wallet in the street with cash blowing all over a four-way intersection. She scurried around scooping up the money, retrieved the wallet, and proceeded to head to the police station to turn it in.

I think every dollar was accounted for.

For years we sent her Christmas cards and offers of free tickets to Disney and our kidney should she ever need it, but we never got to meet this angel who helped us get into Canada—and back home.

Tempting fate, twenty-five years later I did it again.

This time we were driving through Arkansas on the way back from camping out west.

We stopped for gas in Conway and then, because we have the ideal car for camping—a Subaru Outback—we made it deep into Alabama before needing gas again.

I do not think it is called nostalgia when you realize that you have repeated one of the dumbest things in the history of your life.

Sure enough, as I slowly pulled into the gas station, I calmly explained to Sarah that I needed to borrow her credit card.

"Not again . . ." she muttered.

Yes, again.

This time, a pastor of the local prison ministry in central Arkansas saw my wallet in a four-way intersection getting run over by car after car.

He pulled over, retrieved everything he could and proceeded to spend the afternoon contacting security officers at the college where I work who began emailing me that my wallet was in Arkansas.

A few days later, every dollar and every credit card arrived in Florida and my wife has never let me hold my wallet at a gas station again.

She did, however, allow me to take my wallet as I hitchhiked on a busy highway near Gunnison, Colorado.

In 2024 we were rafting with our son Gabriel down the Gunnison River when we realized the keys to the truck that was to take the raft and the rest of us back to the boathouse were—12.1 miles, or more precisely—24,200 footsteps from where his Dodge Ram was parked. We had managed to lock them up safely in our Subaru rather than transport them to where they would be of some use.

When we climbed out of the raft at the end of our trip, Sarah and I discovered a unique feature of Colorado's environment. Despite very low humidity and practically no standing water anywhere, mosquitoes by the billions have decided to make their home there.

The swarms of miniature Count Draculas' that descended upon us created a sort of bizarre mixture of dancing, jumping, and swatting that would have been temporarily funny if not for the fact that we had no transportation to escape them.

So, after managing to avoid hitchhiking for the first fifty-seven-plus years of my life, there I was, walking down highway 50—backward—with my thumb out while Gabriel stayed with his mother and dog and looked up YouTube videos on how to hotwire his truck.

After all, his dad does not own a cell phone, so they had no way of knowing where I was or what progress I was making.

I am not sure if it was because my hitchhiking form looked odd or because I was swatting mosquitoes with great effort with my non-hitchhiking hand, but for some reason no one stopped to give me a ride. In fact, I think they sped up as they drove past me.

I kept thinking that this was discriminatory in some way since had Sarah been the one on the highway, twenty cars would have pulled over within seconds.

Nevertheless, my plan was not working, and I am certain no one was interested in my gender theory of hitchhiking success.

Then it dawned on me that rather than waiting for someone to be a good Samaritan I should just pick a house along the highway and go ask them for a ride.

Just then I looked up and saw a large white van pull into a driveway up ahead on the other side of the busy road.

After sprinting across every lane and the median I made it down another mosquito ditch and to the van as it was stopping.

The guy driving it was the co-pilot of a private jet that flies rich Texans to and from Gunnison.

He was talking to the pilot, who he was supposed to pick up at that moment, when I interrupted, explained my predicament, and offered to pay market prices for a ride. The pilot told him he was not ready to leave yet, and I rejoiced at my good fortune.

It shames me to say this, but up until that moment, as an Oklahoman I had maintained the oath of all Okies to dislike people from the Republic of Texas whether we know them or not.

But here I was, riding in a van with just about the nicest person, or Texan, you could ever meet. He even volunteered great stories from his father's days playing for the Dallas Cowboys and refused to accept any money for his trouble. All the way back to Sarah, Gabriel, and Jake, I kept wondering how I was supposed to talk bad about Texas with people like that living there.

Which brings me to my chance meeting with a guy a lot of people have talked about—and not always in the most flattering way.

Years ago, when we were camping near Jackson, Wyoming, the idea of rafting came up but we did not know anything about the river conditions that summer.

Not wanting to waste money on low water levels, I figured I should find a "local" to fill me in on how much snow and rain this part of the state had received in the past several months.

As I came up on the milk section of the store I saw an elderly man in boots, jeans, a leather vest, a denim shirt, and cowboy hat surveying the dairy options.

I thought, "Bingo. This guy looks like a local."

"Excuse me, sir, can I ask you a question?"

He slowly turned around, and my question did not come out.

"You don't know who I am, do you?" he asked.

"Yes, Vice President Cheney, I know exactly who you are," was my reply while my brain was asking me, "Wait, the former Vice President of the United States goes out to buy his own milk??"

Mr. Cheney and I, along with Sarah, had a pleasant conversation about politics and economics . . . for about five minutes, while I managed to forget to ask him about water levels near Jackson.

Other than that obvious moment, politics is not something I ever seek to discuss while camping, but I have learned that if that subject must come up, Newfoundland is the best place for it to appear.

In all the years we have spent camping, we have discovered that for some strange reason, the people of Canada make the best short-term acquaintances. We have even found that the further we go into eastern Canada, the more Canadians tell us that the friendliest people are farther east.

Newfoundland is as far to the east as you can get, and the several-hour ferry crossing (and requisite nausea) is worth it just to meet the people on this island who think nothing of inviting you to stay at their homes or stop over for tea.

In 2023 we were camping at the Berry Hill campground on the west coast. This location had a very nice common area with two large wood stoves, picnic tables and, unfortunately, Wi-Fi connections.

On dry days we saw people sitting in this spot, heads down, scrolling around on their phones.

But then it started raining—and getting cold—and an amazing thing happened.

Sarah and I decided to build a fire in each stove one morning and have breakfast under a real roof.

In a pretty short period of time, people from all over the campground began filtering in one by one.

To see that public area transformed into a loose collection of friends was one of the highlights of our years as campers.

There was something nearly magical about how the warmth of the fires, along with the rain and randomness of people's arrival, made for hours of great conversations, dining, clothes drying, and laughter.

Being two of the very few Americans present, eventually the subject of politics came up.

Without commenting on the political environment that the United States has been in for years, I will just say that it was so refreshing to sit with calm, polite, respectful people who asked great questions, listened intently, and never lost their temper.

We learned so much about Canadian history and politics. We were able to debate our differences and discuss what was going on in the States without anyone suggesting that we had lost our minds.

And not one Canadian got upset with me when I asked them why their government had not fixed the potholes on Newfoundland's roads that are very similar in size to the craters astronauts find on the moon.

For Sarah, perhaps the most meaningful five-minute friendship she has ever had on our camping adventures came in 2019 as we were hiking near Mt. Hood, in Oregon.

As we were nearing the Timberline Lodge—the place made famous in the movie *The Shining*, Sarah and I began to hear singing off in the distance, but still on our trail. Well, it was not actually singing. It was more like the voice of an opera star from the heavens.

We picked up our pace to see if we could find out where this beautiful voice was and as we rounded a bend we saw her. It was a lady who we learned was in her seventies that had just stopped toward the end of her more than fifty-mile, multiday hike to appreciate the mountains around her with song.

She was a true inspiration to Sarah that life does not need to slow down as we age and that singing with a grateful heart is one way to appreciate what life has to offer.

Disconnecting from Everything

I have never owned a cell phone and never will. I keep track of the news only to the extent that I need to do my job.

I miss Walter Cronkite, so I usually skip the evening news. I do not have any social media accounts and on most days, would rather not know who the President is or what Congress is up to.

I find that being near a great campfire under billions of stars and with people I like to hang out with is a great way to leave the world even further behind.

The best way to make tent camping a genuinely healthy experience is to force yourself to eliminate every part of life that brings you back into the rat race the rest of the planet is in.

If you can completely avoid texting, the news, social media, email, You-Tube, and the other million urban distractions—and tell your employer you are on a literal vacation (derived from the phrase "to vacate everything that is annoying") you will have a great chance to immerse yourself in everything nature is and leave behind a world that is, for the most part, pretty lousy.

You will discover when you get home and turn on the news that you have not missed much. Humans are still humans and will be doing human stuff while you are looking at the Big Dipper and eating marshmallows. This is especially true during global pandemics or election years or when there is social unrest. Far from suggesting that you mimic an ostrich, I am simply suggesting that it is unhealthy to see nothing but panicked people in masks; hear eighty-

Morning in Granite Campground, Almont, Colorado

year-old politicians' blather on about anything, and watch the country grow angrier by the day. Getting away from all of that, from time to time, is medicine for our minds.

One more thing—and this may sound like absurd advice coming from an economist.

Do not wait for your checkbook to indicate you are safe to travel.

When Sarah and I were about to leave for Tennessee on our first long camping trip with our boys, the subject of money came up. At that time, for a variety of reasons, we were stretched thin, like many other American families.

She brought up the idea of maybe tabling our travels and building up our savings so that down the road we would have more of a buffer and eventually a more secure retirement nest egg.

I told her that in retirement I hoped to have enough money for a "rocking chair and a newspaper subscription" and that while we were young, and the boys were at home, I wanted to spend our extra time and money traveling as much as possible.

This meant that early in our marriage and parenthood there were many times that we went off on long camping trips, far from Florida, and even with a little budget book we kept, our finances were not in great shape when we got home.

This meant teaching extra classes, selling more stuff on eBay, writing books, and other things to repair the hole in our bank account. It was worth every penny and by the spring of 2020 we were so grateful that we had made it to forty-seven out of the fifty states and most of Canada.

You can travel relatively cheaply on these trips but if you wait until you have enough money to comfortably afford a long time away then you might look up and realize you are old, your children have moved on, and you do not have the desire for adventure that you might have had while you were younger.

Traveling like the Clampetts

If you are under the age of forty-five there is a good chance you have never watched a classic television show from the 1960s called *The Beverly Hillbillies.* If you go online and find an image of what Jed Clampett and his family's truck looked like on the way to California, that is pretty darn close to what we look like coming home from every camping trip.

On the way out, our SUVs from the past and current Subarus are always a bit lower in back than our shocks and struts would appreciate.

But we always make it to wherever we are going.

It is coming back when the trouble starts, the highway patrol gets involved, and people laugh at us and ask stupid questions. The fun is in the memories of such absurd packing behavior.

After stopping to see my parents in Oklahoma one fall I made two decisions that seemed like good ideas at the time until they became bad ideas.

First, even though it was October, I cut down what was going to be our Christmas tree from their land. That is because, as an economist (a.k.a., a person who is thrifty with money), I hate paying $75 for a tree that is only going to last a couple of weeks. $0 and green spray paint, should it come to that, was a better plan.

Then, I bought a small aluminum boat from my parents that they were no longer using.

First, the Christmas tree was tied to the top of the car. Then, the boat was strapped on top of the Christmas tree, which was so large that it was sticking out from under the boat prominently enough to create comedians all over the south.

When we began our journey back home, every gas stop was met with some version of, "Hey man, Christmas ain't for another two months!" And, of course, people would stare, honk, and laugh as they went past our creatively packed automobile.

In Arkansas, we were pulled over by a highway patrol officer who told us we changed lanes without signaling.

He pulled this nonsense out of the thin air while staring at the tree and boat the entire time. I am certain that he thought I must be ferrying drugs under the tree and the boat. Why else would I have such a combination of nonobvious rooftop decorations?

Driving through Alabama we stopped in Bayou La Batre—not for lunch, or more gas, but because Sarah spotted some saltwater fishing nets by a dumpster and wanted them for some project at home. These nets were enormous. It did not matter.

I took the boat and the Christmas tree off the roof and put the nets on top. Then, the tree was put on the nets and the boat made it back on top of the tree. Our SUV was about 7 feet tall when we left home. It came back looking like a mini-tractor trailer.

The tree turned brown and dried up to something even Charlie Brown would not have liked. The boat was fine once I fixed the leaks I spotted while fishing in an alligator-infested lake, and twenty years after retrieving the fishing nets, Sarah finally found a home for them in her garden.

Sarah is a professional artist and is always looking for things she can use in her pottery and other creations, so I have learned to pull over whenever she says, "pull over."

In Tennessee one Fall I was asked to retrieve birch tree limbs from a river that she needed for some baskets she was making.

Driving through Georgia on the way home she asked me to stop so she could ask a cotton farmer for some bushels of cotton—still on the stalk—from his field. He said yes, so I put the cotton on top of the limbs. That would have been unusual enough except for the fact that while visiting friends in Centerville, Tennessee, she bought a kitchen sink from their store that we tied to the back of the car. I think they sold it to her so they could laugh while saying something along the lines of " . . . everything AND the kitchen sink!"

But even with all her eclectic supply requests she has never overloaded one of our vehicles to the point of blowing out the shocks and causing the front end of our car to point toward the sky.

That honor was mine.

Every time we go to Minnesota or Wisconsin, I bring back one of my favorite drinks of all time—Sprecher's Cream Soda. I used to tell our boys that it was liquid gold for only special occasions in our game room.

One year while everyone was asleep, I drove to Menards and proceeded to buy well over 100 bottles of this delectable beverage. Or maybe it was 200.

I crammed (hid) bottles in every nook and cranny in what was already an extraordinarily back-heavy car.

We made it from Bloomington, Minnesota, to Wildwood, Florida, when we heard a loud banging sound followed by the back of our car sagging to what seemed like an inch off the ground. The front of the car was angled in such a way that I thought this must be what the astronauts in rocket ships see when they are sitting down on the launch pad.

Again, honking and laughing followed us the rest of the way home and then Sarah's question of "What in the world could have caused that?" was answered with each bottle retrieved.

The boys were thrilled that their dad had managed to pull off such a large, and well-hidden, haul.

Kids

Being at camp and seeing kids play with sticks and rocks or building a fort or some other structure is a joy to behold.

They can go on like this for hours and will not interrupt their time by asking to see your phone or watch television. Without the constant interruptions and busyness of normal life we were able to sit with our kids and enjoy far

A good story over coffee—Crab Lake (2008)

more time listening to them or reading *The Hardy Boys*, or fishing. And then there were the miles of hiking. . . .

Taking kids on hikes—even long ones—is a way to get them to value being outside and learn more about animals, plants, and the value of protecting our resources.

When taking long hikes with our boys we discovered that there is something even more practical and effective than verbally encouraging them as they trudge uphill.

Bribery.

When our boys were young, and we ventured out on adult-version hiking trips we knew that their little legs were going to start rebelling at some point. We always told them that if they finished the hike they would get an entire 16-ounce root beer with dinner.

They looked like Sir Edmund Hilary the rest of the day.

During our journeys around the US, we also discovered one of the all-time best ideas our government has come up with. That is the National Park Service Junior Ranger program.

When a youngster signs up for this program, they will be given a book to fill out as they go around the park learning new things. When they are done, they will have a little oath they have to repeat and then they will be given a nice badge from that park.

You will not believe how excited children get when they pin that badge on them.

It also does something else.

Part of being in the Junior Ranger program is the constant reminder to "leave no trace." This means footprints are OK to leave and photos are good to take but nothing else.

Every time we camped anywhere with our boys, I would remind them to leave the campsite better than they found it. This meant going around with them and picking up any pieces of trash that we did not create and visiting the other sites to do the same.

They derived great pride and satisfaction from putting in more effort than would normally be expected, and they quickly saw how careless other people can be.

As they became grown men their innate desire to practice good stewardship did not go away and they were just as conscious of their behavior as adults as they were asked to be as children.

Another one of the great joys of having young children (and sometimes teenagers) along with you is hearing—and attempting to process—the many ridiculously funny things they say as you roll down the highway or when you are relaxing at camp.

A sampling . . .

In Sherbrook, Nova Scotia, Sarah came out of a coffee shop with creamers for our coffee.

Gabriel: "How many creamers did you get?"

Sarah: "Enough for me and Dad."

Gabriel: "Why didn't you get some for me?"

Sarah: "We already discussed this."

Gabriel: "What did we decide?"

In Yellowstone National Park Gehrig started a "sapstick" business in the Bridge Bay campground when he was about six years old.

He picked up pine twigs and dabbed the twigs with sap from trees near our tent.

Then he put all his twigs down on a stump near the road where he informed me that he was going to charge a penny a stick and that he was going to sit there and "wait for the pennies to come by."

While camping in Jasper National Park, Sarah kept working with Gabriel on how to say the word "smoke."

He would always say "moke" so Sarah had him sit on her lap and practice saying smoke over and over again. One morning near the fire Gabe said, "Moke keeps coming this way."

"What did you say?" his mother asked.

Gabriel paused, looked around, and said, "That white stuff keeps coming this way."

Finally, in 2014 we were in the Badlands National Park where Gehrig was complaining about how wet and cold it was. Sarah heard a baby crying nearby and said, "Gehrig, you're fussing just like that baby."

Grinning, he replied, "That baby's got a good point."

Dogs

The year 2014 had been the roughest summer we had ever spent camping together as a family. Gehrig was fifteen and Gabriel was thirteen. If you have had, or do have, teenagers in this age group you will immediately ask, "Why did you go anywhere with them in the back of your car?"

Good question.

We had many wonderful camping moments out west that summer but, teenagers being teenagers, I recall reaching a point somewhere in Washington where I was sitting in a laundromat (another feature of camping) thinking, "I will never travel with these people again."

By the time we were heading east and into Montana, Gehrig, our oldest, put in an unusual, but welcome request.

"Dad, can we skip the Going-to-the-Sun Road this summer?"

I was greatly relieved that he asked that. It gave me just the opening I needed to say to everyone, "Hey, let's skip the curvy, steep, narrow, no guard rails, vertical drop, and often snow-covered road that runs through Glacier National Park."

So, we did.

A day or so later Gabriel and I were sitting near a river discussing a dog he had "won" the summer before.

In 2013 I promised him that if he hit a home run in his last year of little league baseball, I would get him a dog. The year before the promise was for a monkey but thankfully, he did not hit a shot over the fence that season.

But, in 2013 he hit a line-drive home run over the centerfield wall and his teammates, who heard about my promise, were barking like dogs as they celebrated at home plate with him.

At that time, he mentioned that if he got a dog a Golden Retriever would be his choice.

A year had passed, and the promise of a dog had not been fulfilled.

For some reason, that day by the river, we discussed the dog again and I told him if we found one, I thought "Jake" would be a great name.

Somewhere around twenty-two hours later, on the outskirts of Wolf Point, Montana, our family was changed, for the better, and we once again were as close as we had been when the boys were little dudes.

The afternoon of July 11, I had nearly three-fourths of a tank of gas as we drove through the Assiniboine and Sioux Reservation and into Wolf Point. I thought there might not be too many chances to fuel up the rest of the day, so we stopped.

As I was walking in to pay for the gas, I heard my wife say, "He's so cute!"

I did not think she was talking about me, so I did not pay much attention to it.

When I got back outside, Gehrig was holding this little Golden Retriever mix at a level where the puppy was looking right into my eyes.

"So, what is going on?" was my natural question.

No one said a word.

That, of course, means a conspiracy was afoot against the father of this family.

Apparently, a couple at the gas station was trying to give this little three-month-old puppy away to a good home when they spotted my wife, the lady who in her lifetime has brought home multiple cats and dogs from gas stations.

"Just take him," they insisted.

As she was thinking about it, they started walking away with the puppy following them.

She called out to Gehrig to grab him—which he did in about two seconds—then I walked out.

I tried every cost-benefit calculation known to man to explain why taking a puppy 2,270 literal miles back to Florida did not make sense.

All she could keep saying, as she clutched him for dear life, was, "But he's so cute . . . "

Seeing my attempts at logic going nowhere, Gabriel looked at his brother and said, "Gehrig, take the puppy away so mom can think!"

Finally, during what I will admit were far from heartfelt protests (I wanted him too . . .), she said, "Just start driving and we will figure it out as we go."

Ten years have passed since then.

Over that period, Jake has been our wonderful sidekick and appreciative companion whether we are taking him away for the summer, or a trip to the snow he loves in the winter.

When we get to Colorado every summer his nickname is "Bad Ape" because the moment he sees the mountains he starts yelling like an ape.

The ape noises are so loud—and so sudden—that while we were once driving near a scientific research center in Gothic, Colorado, he waited until some skinny guy with a giant afro, carrying what looked like a $500,000 telescope, got right next to our moving car and then erupted like a chimpanzee on espresso.

Sarah and Jake . . . day one

As we drove by, I saw this kid juggling this telescope until he finally secured it, turned around, and glared menacingly at our bad ape.

Our "Jake Dog" as we call him, has been one of the greatest accidents our family has ever experienced, and he has brought more laughter and joy to all of us than we can imagine.

Here's hoping you find a furry stranger at a gas station someday. If you do, try to find a way to say, "OK, let's do this."

Campfires and Cooking Great Food

In addition to stray dogs, new friends, and the departure of technology from our life, there have been other aspects of tent camping that have added great joy to our lives.

First, and perhaps oddly, there is the near primitive pleasure I derive from finding, gathering, and cutting up my own campfire wood.

I can tell you from firsthand experience that there are few things more gratifying than finding all the firewood you will need during your stay. In 2023, out of ninety nights in a tent we managed to spend a grand total of $18 on firewood all because of something George Costanza said about refusing to pay for parking: "Why should I pay for it, when if I apply myself, I might get it for free?"

In many places around the US, it is perfectly legal to gather dead wood off the ground, cut it up, and supply your own fuel for cooking and keeping warm.

In other places you will see the dreaded signs telling you about permits.

Without making any overt suggestions I will just mention that these signs are not common and not far from these warnings are places with <u>no</u> signs. Where there are no signs . . . Well, you get the idea.

But there is another great source of free wood that will not make you appear to be a lawbreaker to anyone. Strange, yes. But not a lawbreaker.

This tactic requires paying close attention to campers in your vicinity who appear to be breaking down their site to leave.

George Costanza was right . . .

Rather than bother them at a time when they are not having any fun, I just hang out nonchalantly in our campsite until the last person from their camp is in their car.

Immediately, I walk (jog if I smell fellow frugal campers closing in) and gather every piece of wood left behind. You will be amazed how many people shell out big bucks for firewood and just abandon it when they are heading home.

When it comes to cooking, we have discovered that if you are cooking steak, or chicken, or pork, letting the larger pieces of wood burn down to a good pile of coals then pouring a high-quality charcoal on top is a great idea.

When we are making eggs, pancakes, or other foods that cannot be placed on the grill, we make sure that we have our reliable old griddle on hand. For these meals we do not use charcoal but still let the larger pieces of wood burn until only the coals remain.

One dinner we enjoy is what we call "cowboy meal." I use canned corn beef hash (do not look at the ingredients) and over melted butter, slowly cook the hash until it is brown. I then push the hash to one side of the griddle and then fry eggs on the other side. Each plate has corned beef hash on the bottom, topped with however many eggs you want on top. It is a memorable meal of genuine camping comfort food.

Now for the chili recipe.

For the best results, make this at home (since it takes six to eight hours). Then, freeze it and take it with you camping. You can then put a little water in a large chili pot and reheat it.

I hope you enjoy the following recipe. If you are from Texas, please do not be offended by the name of this meal. But you Texans will appreciate one deleted ingredient you <u>never</u> put in chili . . .

Jack's Oklahoma Chili Recipe

4 lbs. grass-fed beef (85% lean) or some combination of grass-fed beef and either venison (preferred) or bison. For this amount, use at least 75% beef.

2–3 medium to large SWEET yellow onions, chopped. The onion is critical so do not use white or red.

In a large pot, brown the meat and onions. Make sure you have some water (a few ounces) to keep the meat from cooking too fast. You may need to add a little water a few times. Cook on high until the meat is brown, or near brown. DO NOT DRAIN THE FAT

Add a 29-ounce can of Hunt's tomato sauce (do not use tomato paste or stewed tomatoes), and the following:

- 9 tablespoons of Chili powder
- 2 tablespoons of garlic powder
- 1 tablespoon of paprika
- 4 tablespoons of crushed cumin
- ½–¾ tablespoons of cayenne pepper (adjusting to your heat tolerance)
- At least 2–3 tablespoons of salt (more, or less, to your tastes is OK)
- 8 tablespoons of LIGHT brown sugar (do not use dark or white sugar)
- A dash of the following (one or two shakes of the bottle . . .): dill, oregano, and basil. You can (and I usually do) add a touch of black pepper.

Important note—If you plan to have the chili for dinner, make sure it is cooking for at least 6–8 hours before. Once all the ingredients are in the pot, turn it to low/simmer and check on it frequently. You should also make sure to stir the pot often to bring meat from the bottom up to the top and have all the spices evenly mixed.

One more thing—Adjusting the sugar content (adding a little more) will take a little of the spicy edge off if you have people who do not like spicy.

And one more thing—DO NOT EVER PUT BEANS IN CHILI! It is a sin against mankind.

There is one more part of cooking and eating that you may never experience, but if you do it will make you a very grateful human being.

That is when you are miles and miles away from anything and have run out of food . . .

This happened to us in 2016.

We had packed our food rations based on our past trips to the BWCA. Previously, the fishing had been fantastic, and our boys were younger, so they ate significantly less food. On this trip we woke up on the morning of our last day of camping only to discover an empty food bag.

Portaging and canoeing all day with no calories were out of the question since we had not eaten since the night before. So, in the sort of declaration a father might have made back in 1852, I looked at everyone and said, "Folks, if we do not catch fish today, we do not eat."

Fishing for Walleye and Northern Pike is great fun and makes for spectacular dining when you are on vacation. Fishing to not starve for a whole day (we were not into fasting of any kind) takes on a whole new meaning—and urgency.

While Gehrig left us to find berries, Gabriel, Sarah, and I fanned out over the shoreline and went to work.

Sometime between lunch and dinner one of us landed a super-nice Pike and between that and the blueberries it was perhaps the most gratifying meal I have ever had.

Campfire Stories

When it comes to sitting around the campfire after dinner, I learned to be careful about the stories I tell. Sometimes it is best just to sit and stare at the fire and watch the flames do their hypnotic dance rather than invite little invaders into our campsite.

One evening, I got the great idea to tell our boys about a little creature called a Hob Goblin that lives in the woods.

I could have won a prize for the picture I created in their minds.

I was very detailed about these little guys, only a few inches tall, that wore big hats like old pirates wore and how they smoked little cigarettes and had knives in their little belts and so on. The kids thought it was amazing that Hob Goblins went wherever they wanted and were kind of troublemakers who came into campsites to plunder and play pranks.

Then, we went to bed.

I swear, that night, Hob Goblins showed up.

While my sons slept soundly, I know I heard a whole regiment of Hob Goblins outside our tent, scratching, running, and yes, laughing. I kept looking for the glow of cigarettes and for the tips of little knife blades.

I was up off and on all night, and, as usual, there were no other campers around that I could sit up with to calm my nerves.

Hiking

If you want to have great satisfaction, for years, bypass the expensive trekking poles (if you can safely do so) and produce your own hiking stick.

I make hiking sticks in Colorado from the limbs of pine trees that have succumbed to beetle kill. The pattern in the wood is stunning. First, find a branch that you can cut to mid-shoulder height.

Then take a good knife and whittle away the bark and any other protrusions. Use fine sandpaper and work the entire stick until it is smooth.

Find a rock with a smooth surface and rub it along the stick to "bone" it and make the grains harder. Then, using a cheap paintbrush and Brazilian Rose Wood oil, lightly coat the stick. Wait twenty minutes, wipe off the excess oil and you are done.

Having a stick you make for yourself will add great pleasure to your hikes and will get you nice comments along the trail.

When packing for your trip follow the experts online or in your hiking survival book to the letter. You will read about water, sunblock, first aid kits, and more. Just do it.

Do not pack too much food or other items you will have no possible use for.

In our early days of hiking my sons liked to joke that Sarah had a Cobra bite kit in her pack when we were 10,000 miles from India.

Sure enough, one day she showed us a snake bite kit on a hike where you are more likely to see Bigfoot than a serpent.

Another great idea is to make sure you get to your trailhead early and pack river shoes if there is any possibility of water crossings on your hike.

You never know when the weather might turn ugly and force you to take shelter for hours. The last thing you want is to copy my mistake at Angleworm Lake in Minnesota and start out on a fourteen-mile hike—near lunchtime— only to have rain, darkness, and poor trail markings lead to the thought of covering my family with pine straw for the night to keep from freezing.

After spending the last two miles drinking rainwater from our ponchos and stumbling over rocks and through mud, we decided to pay more attention to the people who hike—and time—these trails.

As for river shoes, I have learned the hard way the consequences of leaving these behind—and encouraging others to do the same.

Sarah would pack these shoes if she was walking across the Sahara Desert. I would probably leave them at camp if we were preparing to walk through, well, multiple rivers and streams.

The one time she let me talk her out of bringing her river shoes we came upon—you guessed it—a river crossing in New Brunswick that was about 100 yards long, across painful rocks, with a rope to help you avoid floating away.

By the time we made it across I was in really big, "I told you so" trouble.

Two days later, she brought these padded shoes on a hike that I was certain had no river crossings until we came upon a river crossing.

She walked across like Moses through the Red Sea and then sat and relaxed as she watched me say "Ouch" repeatedly, barefooted, and stupidly.

But thanks to Clint Eastwood, my stupidity has limits.

In the movie *Magnum Force*, Clint Eastwood famously said, "A man has got to know his limitations."

Live by this when you are planning any hiking trip.

In 2024, my friend Kirk (the guy who thought the devil was with us forty years earlier), invited me to go on a camping and hiking trip to the Grand Canyon.

The original plan was to get backcountry permits and spend three to four days trekking through an area I have never seen before.

When we failed to secure permits for the dates we needed, another idea came up.

Kirk has had, for quite some time, a sort of "bucket list" item that involves a rim-to-rim-to-rim Grand Canyon hike that covers more than forty-four miles in one day.

Apparently, this is actually a thing people do, and at the age of fifty-seven, temporary insanity came over me and I said, "Let's do it."

Kirk is the manager of a large gym near Dallas and works out in preparation for things like this.

I mow my yard in Florida once a week and hike a lot of five-to-ten-mile jaunts during the summer.

"Have you taken complete leave of your senses?" is what I think I heard Sarah say to me as I bounded upstairs to do more research on this upcoming marathon into the bowels of Arizona.

Twenty minutes later I emailed Kirk and told him what Clint Eastwood once said.

For some odd reason the internet was full of dire warnings specifically aimed at fifty-seven-year-old men who have taken leave of their senses. Reading about how helicopters do not come to give you water or take you out in case your once-a-week lawn mowing schedule was not adequate preparation, was enough to restore good sense to my brain.

6

A Place for Healing and Reflection

In August of 1998 I was in a parking lot close to a trail where mountain climbers begin their trek to the top of Mt. Rainier, in Washington.

Sarah and I had risen at 5 a.m. that morning and managed to hike to more than 10,000 feet, in almost complete solitude, until the snow fields indicated that we needed to turn around.

In that parking lot was a man, probably in his fifties, with his two grown sons.

As I watched them put their gear on, I reflected for a moment on how wonderful that must feel for that father to have his boys with him.

I looked at Sarah and told her that I was going to do that with my two sons someday.

On that August day she was three months pregnant, and we did not yet know that we were going to have a boy—our first—on February 4, 1999.

Gehrig William Chambless was an almost perfect child.

From infancy he was always smiling, bright-eyed, and eager to see what each day would bring.

When we took him camping, for the first time, he was about six months old. He had a little bassinet that he slept in and would wake up every morning in Idaho, or Wyoming, or Montana with bright eyes and a big smile that resembled some of the ants in the movie "A Bug's Life." Sarah even took to calling him the "Bugs life baby."

We would put him in the infant carrier pack that we had borrowed and took him everywhere we went hiking.

Every time we would come to a waterfall, he would peak around my shoulder and intently watch the water cascading down.

He even had his first taste of sugar on a camping trip.

When we got to the old lodge in Yellowstone near Old Faithful, we stopped off for some ice cream. We were told that huckleberries were their specialty and after a bit of coaxing I got Sarah to relax her plans to keep sugar away for his first year of life and let him try this western treat.

He devoured it with a ferocity that was shocking and hilarious . . .

On October 21, 2000, Gehrig's little brother Gabriel joined our family.

From the time he was in Sarah's womb he was a fighter.

When Sarah was about two months from delivering him, she developed a medical condition that led her doctor to recommend having an abortion.

She refused and both she and Gabriel made it through his delivery in fine shape. His blonde hair and big laugh made him quite popular everywhere Sarah took him.

In July and August of 2019, I fulfilled my promise to Sarah and began putting on my gear, with my grown sons, to begin a forty-six-mile backcountry camping trip in Mt. Rainier National Park.

This was the hardest physical challenge I have ever experienced.

If you are familiar with Mt. Rainier, we hiked from the Carbon River entrance to Ipsut Creek on July 31. On August 1, we made it to James Camp. From there we hiked to Berkeley Park, Dick Creek Camp, and Eagle's Roost Camp on August 4 before arriving at Mowich Lake.

As usual, I could not believe how heavy a backcountry pack could be. I also did not understand how all forty-six miles could be straight uphill, or so it seemed.

On the third day of our journey it rained, nonstop, with biting temperatures all day long. The fog and river crossings added to the difficulty and of course our packs were soaked, even with rain gear covering them.

That night we were all sound asleep by 7 p.m., exhausted and a bit concerned about the temperatures that were coming.

We laid out our wet clothes, hoping they might dry a little overnight.

When we woke up, they had a layer of ice over them. It was thin, but it was still ice.

That morning, we ate one of our last dehydrated meals that normally we would not have been excited about. This "breakfast skillet" was bad, but it was warm and so we felt like we were dining at the Ritz Carlton.

When we put on our socks, we knew we were in trouble. Our feet were so cold it was hard not to shake uncontrollably. That is when Gehrig launched what I called the "Toe Glove" idea. He had the thought of first putting our feet in zip lock bags and then pulling our frozen socks and wet hiking boots over that.

It worked like a charm.

Weeks later as he and Sarah would share their semi-nightly ritual of watching *Shark Tank,* I would ask Gehrig, "Say, when are you going to make your Toe Gloves?" He was working on it, he would answer.

Perhaps the hardest part of the Rainier trip was the sheer number of switchbacks we (I) had to endure.

The boys would get four or five switchbacks ahead of me and I would wearily call up to them and ask, "Is that it?" Each time they would slowly shake their head "No" and I would proceed.

Often, as I would turn a corner, I would see Gehrig standing there. He was always sporting a genuine and somewhat goofy grin on his face, and I think my efforts to conquer this trail were admirable to him.

We would sit and talk for a few minutes while I rested. He would always ask if I was alright and away we would go. Then it would be Gabriel waiting for me and telling me I was almost there, wherever "there" was.

There was one instance however where Gehrig was not as sympathetic but was funny.

At one point on day 4, I think, I was feeling light-headed, dizzy, and short of breath. I started to seriously consider the possibility of having a heart attack since I had never felt that weird before.

I motioned for the boys to come back down to me where I sat down and began telling them what I wanted them to do if I did indeed fail to make it.

At some point I said to Gehrig, "And Gehrig, when you get home you just sell off my entire eBay store and give your mother 80 percent of the money." Looking back, his response was hilarious. . . .

"Wait, why does Mom get 80 percent?" was his question as Gabriel looked at him with slightly raised eyebrows.

Of course, this was all my fault for raising him to be a good capitalist. The way he figured it, he was going to have to do all the work so why shouldn't he get a bigger cut?

But at that moment, all I could think was, "Man, your dad just told you that he thinks he is going to have a heart attack."

On the last night of the trip, we came across a rare human being camping near us.

It was a young woman, by herself, who was happy to have some company. At one point she asked us about the food we had brought on this trip.

When I started talking about tuna and salmon packs, nuts, and so forth she began shaking her head and saying, "No, no, no. . . ."

Her next quote is one I have lived by ever since when hiking anywhere—even two blocks down to our post office.

"Eat shit, stay fit."

She told us we should have been eating corn chips and other high carb, fast burning junk that would give us energy and not allow our blood to spend so much time digesting. This insight left us all a little more excited about future hiking snacks even though I forgot to ask her if that included Peach Nehi.

Thank you, young lady, whoever you are.

The next morning, Gabriel discovered an amazing feature of Eagle's Roost. "Dad, you have _got_ to check this out!" echoed behind him as he bounded down into our camp.

The pit toilet at this camp is mounted on a high rock like a king's throne overlooking a breathtaking valley. It is even called "the throne" by hikers in this area. I left that morning wondering how to get something like that installed on the roof of my house.

That afternoon, Mt. Rainier emerged from the clouds. It felt like we could reach out and touch it. The blue of the glaciers and the majestic features had us standing in awe for what seemed like forever.

Gabriel and Gehrig Chambless Mt. Rainier National Park (August 2019)

As we descended, we walked past a huge field of snow—probably 150 yards long—that was gently sloping away from the trail.

I made it past this field and was planning to keep walking when this very subtle feeling came over me that we should go back and slide down this hill.

We took turns, repeatedly, climbing to the top of the snow field, taking off in a dead sprint, getting into a perfect baseball slide and flying down the snow.

I think we all felt like little kids again and to this day I enjoy watching the videos of this detour.

That night, as we ended our journey, we stopped in Wilkeson, Washington (population 488) at the Pick & Shovel Saloon and Restaurant. The restaurant had just closed, and you could not, per state law, go into the bar unless you were twenty-one.

But we were starving.

So, when I walked into the bar with my twenty- and eighteen-year-old sons I was naturally asked, "Are they 21?"

To this day I think it is the only bald face lie my boys ever heard me say.

The bartender offered to serve us food and to this day it might have been the greatest meal of my life. I would also be willing to bet his tip was the biggest he has ever received.

Thank you, sir, whoever you are. . . .

Within a day or so, Sarah joined us in Oregon for a week of great laughing, hiking, and reminiscing about the special times we had experienced along the Oregon coast years ago.

Sometime in mid-August we took the boys to Portland International Airport. Gehrig had started a small business he needed to tend to, and Gabriel had to go back to work.

When Sarah and I hugged them on the sidewalk that warm Oregon afternoon we did not know that it would be the last time our family would ever travel together.

Tragically and unexpectedly, Gehrig died on April 26, 2020.

Writing about it at this moment, it is still completely unfathomable that he is gone.

To know Gehrig was to conclude that he would probably be elected President of the United States someday. I know I had that thought more than once and shared the sentiment with him.

He was a superstar of a human being and in every other way as well.

An Honorable Mention All-American baseball player and star football player in high school, he was recruited by schools all over America in both sports and as a college student he managed to compile over 80 credits with all A's and just one B.

The people he worked for thought he was just about the most humble, kind, and hardworking kid they had ever seen.

They were right.

No request of him was ever too burdensome and no situation was too far removed from his gentle spirit and great laugh. He rarely complained about anything.

In the more than twenty-one years Sarah and I were lucky enough to have him, we got to see a smiling, happy, exceedingly thoughtful boy and young man who told great stories and was adored and loved by his many friends. He and Gabriel were practically inseparable and enjoyed years of imaginative, joyful, and adventurous times together as brothers and best friends.

On our many trips as a family Gehrig would, when he was young, pretend to be the pioneer, David Crockett, while Gabriel was his sidekick, Georgie Russell. He would tell us an endless array of stories from the back seat of the car as we traveled down the road.

As a younger man his favorite pastime was writing songs, stories, and poetry that revealed a creative and thoughtful side of him that few people knew about.

Like other parents who lose a child, we were—and still are—left with so many questions and piercing grief that never goes away.

There is simply no possible way to put into words what it means to have a child die when it appeared he was at the beginning of great things and a great life.

But we have discovered—and want to offer this suggestion to anyone reading this that is struggling with loss—that being in nature is the single most helpful treatment we have found.

Since the summer of 2020 we have packed our gear and left for Colorado too many times to count. We have revisited the Boundary Waters and spent months in Canada in 2023.

Every time we leave Florida behind and set up our tent somewhere—anywhere—in nature we feel that we are incrementally improving.

That is not to say that there have not been numerous occasions where we feel devastated, alone, and beside ourselves with grief. We have seen our perspective on God change dramatically and relationships with many of our friends change as a result of our loss.

On more than one occasion I have been out on trails and have wondered what it would be like if I peered into the forest and saw Gehrig walking slowly toward me with his infectious grin. The imagery is so real that it is almost like a dream. I can see him coming closer and nodding or waving. Then, the image goes away, and I am left with the rest of my life without him. It is that part—the rest of our lives—that being in nature helps us process.

There is something incredibly profound to look around you in a panoramic display of wonder and contemplate life and all the people who have come before us and will come after us who have had to experience loss on this scale. To stare up at the stars and concentrate your mind on the vastness of the universe and how short our time on the planet is, is humbling. Nature has an incredible way, especially if you spend a long time in it, to remind you of how fleeting and simultaneously wonderful life really is.

Sunset over Lake Tenkiller near Park Hill, Oklahoma

We have found, in nature, that perhaps the best any of us can hope to do is to live our lives in as much peace and joy as possible and to be kind to all living beings. We have concluded that the little ant struggling on the ground is important because it is alive and that if all we leave behind is a legacy of trying to do good then perhaps that is enough.

We both know that in his twenty-one years, two months, and twenty-two days our son left that legacy and that it will be impactful to other people, in one way or another, for eternity.

When we are home and surrounded by reminders of what our little family used to be it is very hard not to be depressed and dysfunctional.

We must fight, every day, to be the kind of people Gehrig would hope we would be while being parents and friends to his resilient, loving, and incredibly considerate younger brother.

Gabriel has had the same drive and fight in him to live his life to the fullest that he had when he was in Sarah's womb and was written off.

It is in large part his strength, optimism, generosity, appreciation for life—and his determination to remain connected to his roots in nature—that has helped us realize that the more time we can spend in sunshine, fresh air, beautiful surroundings, and the solitude it creates, the more we will be able to come to terms with the fact that our family has radically changed and we have to make a decision to live, love, and endure.

Today, Gabriel splits his time between work on a ranch that looks like it is in Austria and serving as a very popular whitewater rafting guide. He tells us that when he is out there amongst the elk, flowers, and Aspen trees, or on the river, it feels like heaven. His warm smile and cheerful spirit make us believe that it is true.

If you are currently struggling with grief, please do yourself a favor and find a way to get away. Even if it is close to your home, there are places out there where you can find some peace and clarity and hope.

The key is to get out there—and keep going out there as much as you can.

And perhaps take a tent along with you from time to time . . .

THE LONELY TAVERN
By Gehrig William Chambless

The lonely tavern on the road
Where weary souls might rest
Its splintered door and rotting floor
Are farthest from the best
The creak with every blast
The whipping of the wind
And not a man forgets its scene
In places he has been

The snow will fall, its sheets of white
Coat the barren road
The freezing storm and biting gale
Is all this place has known
From mountain rest, upon the road
It lies between the worlds
Where strangers pass it every night
Going to and fro

The fire burning softly glows
Beckons to its warmth
The streaks of light, dance about
Through the broken door

The black and white and coldest night
Colder than the last
The lonely tavern on the road
Calls to all who pass

The sailor who's return to home
The first in many months
The preacher who will always go
Searching for his flock
The foreigner in the silly hat
Who cannot say a word
Of the language that they speak
That he never got to learn

The outlaw in the corner
Who's always on the run
His eyes darting back and forth
His hand still on his gun
The lady in black, whose husband died
Who's left to go back east
And the tiny boy with his single toy
No shoes upon his feet

The sailor curses the cursed storm
The preacher bows to pray
The foreigner gives his silly hat
To the boy who wants to play
The widow in black drifts to sleep
The first she's had in years
And the outlaw sitting in the corner
Forgets his every fear

The kind man standing behind the bar
Pouring each their drink
Whiskey, milk, or coffee black
He meets their every need
This shelter from the fiercest storm
The kind man has built
But no one ever heard his name
And no one ever will

So many roads have come to cross
That will never meet again
Each will go their separate way
Each pursues its end
But in a world of freezing storms
Each of them will know
There's a little bit of kindness at
The lonely tavern on the road

www.ingramcontent.com/pod-product-compliance
Lightning Source LLC
Chambersburg PA
CBHW070816170726
48000CB00017B/924